WELCOME TO *Haunted* LAS VEGAS NEVADA

Tracie Austin-Peters

Schiffer Publishing Ltd

4880 Lower Valley Road, Atglen, Pennsylvania 19310

Other Schiffer Books on Related Subjects:
Scare-Izona, 978-0-7643-2844-2, $14.95
Coastal Ghosts of Southern California, 978-0-7643-3150-3, $14.99
Haunts of Western Oregon, 978-0-7643-3224-1, $14.99
Mid-Century Vegas, 1930s to 1960s, 978-0-7643-3129-9, $39.99

*Ouija Board is a registered trademark of Parker Brothers Games.

Schiffer Books are available at special discounts for bulk purchases for sales promotions or premiums. Special editions, including personalized covers, corporate imprints, and excerpts can be created in large quantities for special needs. For more information contact the publisher:

Published by Schiffer Publishing Ltd.
4880 Lower Valley Road
Atglen, PA 19310
Phone: (610) 593-1777; Fax: (610) 593-2002
E-mail: Info@schifferbooks.com

For the largest selection of fine reference books on this and related subjects, please visit our web site at:

www.schifferbooks.com

We are always looking for people to write books on new and related subjects. If you have an idea for a book please contact us at the above address.

This book may be purchased from the publisher. Include $5.00 for shipping. Please try your bookstore first. You may write for a free catalog.

In Europe, Schiffer books are distributed by
Bushwood Books
6 Marksbury Ave.
Kew Gardens
Surrey TW9 4JF England
Phone: 44 (0) 20 8392 8585; Fax: 44 (0) 20 8392 9876
E-mail: info@bushwoodbooks.co.uk
Website: www.bushwoodbooks.co.uk

Library of Congress Control Number: 2009927562

Designed by Stephanie Daugherty
Type set in Futura Bk BT/NewsGoth BT

ISBN: 978-0-7643-3286-9
Printed in China

Dedication

To all those in search of the paranormal...
those I have met and those I have yet to meet

Acknowledgments

There are a number of people who I would like to give special thanks to from the bottom of my heart. Without them this book would not have become a reality.

Firstly, to my new found paranormal friend's—*the Las Vegas Society of Supernatural Investigations* (LVSSI)—for their first-hand true ghost accounts!

I would also like to thank Dinah Roseberry and Schiffer Publishing for giving me the opportunity to write this book, and my editor Jennifer Marie Savage for all her hard work.

To Nick Roy for his personal ghost experience mentioned in the introduction, and a big hearted thank you to my artist Christine Dennett for her commitment to this project and her amazing ability to illustrate the unseen.

I would also like to thank my parents for accepting my paranormal obsession over these many years, and to my husband for his much appreciated support.

Last but certainly by no means least, to the highest source of all—for giving us an afterlife to investigate.

Note to the Reader

The following ghost cases that you are about to read are all true accounts. *Welcome to Haunted Las Vegas, Nevada* takes you on a journey of firsthand ghostly investigations as researched and documented by LVSSI—*Las Vegas Society of Supernatural Investigations*. But while the events are true, names of the people involved have been changed to protect their privacy, as some of the cases reveal how the lives of these ordinary people were turned upside down through the interaction of the unknown. I only ask that you keep an open heart and an open mind as you join me on this Las Vegas ghostly journey!

Contents

Foreword

If you're looking for a collection of real life ghost investigation cases, then you've come to the right place! As an avid and passionate researcher of the paranormal side of life, Tracie Austin-Peters has carefully put together over a dozen ghost investigation accounts that will both shock and fascinate you!

I have known Tracie for many years and know her to be passionate and committed to the paranormal side of life.

I myself am a spiritualist medium living in the United Kingdom, and have had many experiences with the paranormal. For example, one day I was called to a friend's house where all of a sudden strange things began to occur. Their dog would start to bark at 3 a.m. every morning, and the strings on the familys' guitar were often heard being plucked! On my investigation, two children from the spirit world, a brother and sister, had arrived from the Victorian era (this was an old Victorian property) and had starved to death as their food was limited, and they were part of a large family.

The spirit children were happy and intrigued to find a dog at this house, along with the guitar and so decided to stay there. Later I was asked to relay this story to a television channel here in England, where I also took the friend's dog from the house along to the studio as well. It's important to understand that pets are very sensitive to the paranormal, and probably more so than humans.

I hope you enjoy reading the following chapters in this ghost book, and find it to be an eye-opener of the paranormal world.. Just remember that nothing is ever what it seems to be...and we are never alone.

Lesley Shepherd, Spiritualist Medium
www.lesleyshepherd-medium.com

Introduction

Ghosts! Most people like to hear a good classic ghost story no matter where the source of the story originates, and over the years I have heard plenty of them. It appears that more and more people around the world are now showing an avid interest and a belief in the ghost phenomena; becoming more aware of their own surroundings and with whom they might be sharing their space. A recent poll revealed that a total of forty-one percent of people believe in ghosts—and as many as sixty-nine percent believe in the survival of the soul after death.

As a child I believed in ghosts, even though at the time I had no real experiences of my own. But for some reason there was always a knowing, a gut feeling that the paranormal realm does indeed exist. But how does one prove the existence of a ghost? As we all know, tangible evidence can often be hard to come by. What is a ghost? What is a spirit? What is the paranormal realm? The meaning of the word paranormal is often referred to as a phenomenon that is not scientifically explainable, a phenomenon that cannot be explained by natural laws. It's also known as the supernatural.

For me, there has never been anything *paranormal* about the subject of the paranormal; on the contrary, I've always considered it to be very much normal. It's part of our everyday world and exists right here with us. There are moments however when our two worlds inter-mingle... when a metamorphosis of energies allows the connection with the spirit, sometimes coming through as a sensing of a spirit's presence, or the hearing of a disembodied voice, or even seeing the spirit of a person in a dream, perhaps seeing the figure of a shadow person out of the corner of your eye, or—if one is lucky enough—seeing the actual physical appearance of the ghost in full form.

Let's talk about what a ghost is for a moment. A simple way to define it is that a ghost is the spirit of a person who was once alive. Everyone eventually passes into the spiritual realm after death, but *not* everyone becomes a ghost. It appears that some people remain as earthbound ghosts and refrain from crossing over into their new existence, as they still have unresolved or unfinished business here on the earthly plain and refuse to accept the light in order to cross over.

It's also said that ghosts are the spirits of people who have died tragically or unexpectedly, and do not accept the reality of their death. This can be a very challenging situation for the ghost and often requires intervention, a helping hand usually from a psychic medium or a powerful individual who knows how to handle the situation correctly, enabling the roaming spirit to accept its death by asking it to walk towards the light and embrace it. Only at this point can they then release their ties from the mortal world.

In past conversations with a number of spiritualist mediums, they have often conveyed to me that it can be somewhat difficult for a spirit to manifest itself and appear as their previous physical earthly form, as a great deal of energy is required to manipulate its surroundings to do this. It perhaps raises the question then of why a ghost would make the decision to physically appear? I remember hearing Mary Ann Winkowski (the *ghost buster* as she's referred to) speaking as a guest on the "Coast to Coast" radio show about her involvement with the television series "Ghost Whisperer," which was inspired in part by her life growing up as a spirit communicator. During the show, she mentioned a number of interesting things, one of which was that a person is more likely to encounter ghost activity around a full moon, as this gives the ghost an abundance of energy and power to come through. Another intriguing comment was that the spirit of a deceased person actually shows up at his or her own funeral! The main reason for this being that the deceased person's relatives and friends are all gathered together to share their most treasured and fondest moments of when the person was alive. I have heard a number of cases like this where people have reported seeing their deceased relative or friend actually standing by their own coffin!

There are a number of ways that spirits try to communicate with us, one of which can be as simple as showing their presence in our dreams. Another way is through the use of electro-magnetic devices such as EMF detectors and various electronic sensors; dowsing rods—the oldest form of divination known to man; cameras and videos; and tape recording machines, which record EVPs known as Electronic Voice Phenomena. EVPs are spirit voices captured on tape that are inaudible to the human ear at the time of the recording. But believe it or not, one very common method for spirits to communicate is through the use of the telephone. I have heard so many reports involving this form of communication; usually what the person hears on the other end of the line is severe static, or a few faint words caught in the midst of the noise. I spoke with a gentleman whose deceased brother called him on the telephone one day and actually said three distinct words to him, "Nick, it's okay." Immediately Nick dialed the appropriate call back number to return the call to his deceased brother, but there was complete silence on the line.

I have personally experienced *this kind of* phenomenon myself, actually twice—on the day of my wedding in Las Vegas and then a day later in California. A total of five calls were made, three of them were in thirty minute intervals throughout the early hours of the morning, and not a soul on the other end of the line except for that of a loud, crackling static! After asking the hotel staff at the front desk if someone was trying to connect a call to our hotel room, we were shocked to hear that no calls were ever incoming to us. What was extremely bizarre about this contact was that the day before in Las Vegas, the first time it had happened, the telephone in the hotel room was actually disconnected from the socket as our personal laptop computer was in use. There was no feasible explanation for this, and after speaking with an acclaimed spiritualist medium friend of mine in England about this bizarre event, she conveyed to me that it was my deceased grandparents trying to 'get through' to wish me luck on my wedding day!

I remember very clearly back in 1987 as a student in London, England, I had my first and only ghost sighting to date, which I am glad to say was also witnessed by another person, a close friend of mine. We had witnessed the materialization of this ghost—a woman dressed in modern day clothing appeared right in front of our very eyes! What was really strange and somewhat disturbing about this ghostly encounter was the fact that she was headless, and as she was seated in front of an entire wall of mirror, her bodily image was not reflected in it. Why was this so, and why was she able to manifest her entire body but no head? Perhaps it would have been a little more acceptable had she have been carrying it under her arm, but no, not a head in sight... completely sans lid! Now many years later, we often recall that mentally challenging encounter, still amazed and yet somewhat privileged to have been witness to her appearance.

What you are about to read in the following chapters is a collection of true and fascinating ghost accounts that were personally investigated by LVSSI—*the Las Vegas Society of Supernatural Investigations*, a team of four extremely credible and dedicated people whose mission it is to help residents of Las Vegas rid their homes of their unwelcome ghostly guests.

Do *you* believe in ghosts? Have you ever seen one, or know of someone who has? Let me tell you that ghosts are indeed very real, and I welcome the opportunity of seeing another in my lifetime. Come and join me on this truly fascinating ghostly journey, to explore the reality of ghosts—*Welcome to Haunted Las Vegas, Nevada!* A super hot, dry, enchanting desert that is home to many a ghostly visitor!

From left-to-right: LVSSI Investigators Tina Carlson, Nancy Riggs, Matthew Winn and Steve Carlson

About LVSSI

Their Mission Statement

LVSSI was founded on the basic principle that individuals need answers and help with the supernatural. Its main goal is to supply these needs to individuals. They are dedicated to offering the most up-to-date knowledge, utilizing field research as well as other groups' field research. They do this as safely as possible, making the client's peace of mind their main objective.

The Investigators

LVSSI is a team that doesn't usually turn down any investigation, but should the strange activity turn out to be more than paranormal—involving, for example, a *demonic* source—they then hand the family over to another credible investigator who is well qualified to help them with that type of a situation; after all, the demonic realm is far different than the ghostly one. A possible example of this appears in the "Our Cemetery" chapter, but as you'll see, in most of their cases they've had a high success rate. Let's meet the team.

Tina Carlson: Founder and director of the Las Vegas Society of Supernatural Investigations that formed in 2000, Carlson says she started LVSSI "because there was no other organization in Las Vegas or surrounding areas for people who were experiencing ghostly activity in their homes to turn to.

"I chose likeminded people for LVSSI and taught them everything I know. I also keep them updated with new theories, policies, and procedures that are constantly changing in the field of the paranormal."

She was also co-director for the Shadowlands Ghosts and Hauntings website for over twelve years. The Shadowlands is a clearinghouse for all things paranormal where people from all over the world seek answers to their questions concerning ghosts as well as many other subjects. LVSSI and Shadowlands will continue to offer this service free-of-charge for as long as there is a need for answers.

Carlson investigates private homes, suspected public hauntings, and cemeteries. "It's my goal to help people find a natural cause for their suspected haunting, or teach them to live peacefully in their own home without fear. I am mostly an empathic—feeling a spirits emotions and frame of mind—and have been known to walk into a suspected haunting and burst into tears or even laughter, due to the spirits emotional energy."

Carlson has also written several articles for Shadowlands based on her research and investigations that have been reprinted on the Internet and in newspapers all over North America, including "Communicating with Ghosts," "Children and Ghosts," and "Common Misconceptions of Ghosts and Haunting's."

Nancy Riggs: An assistant director with LVSSI, Riggs has been actively pursuing the paranormal for over six years. "It has been one of the most fascinating experiences of my life."

Riggs adds, "For three generations my family has been interested in the paranormal and so this curiosity is quite natural for me. As a child living in Alaska and here in Las Vegas Nevada, we have had spirits living with us. It was very normal to talk to, smell, and feel their presence around my family. With Las Vegas Society of Supernatural Investigations, I feel that we can prove to the best of our ability that spirits do co-exist with us. We can give knowledge, comfort, and understanding to those families that seek our help, as it is hard for them to live with something that they feel is harmful, scary, and a nuisance.

Matthew Winn: Assistant director of LVSSI, Winn has lived in Las Vegas, Nevada, all his life. He's married and has two children. "I became interested in paranormal investigation when I was sixteen. I grew up hearing the family ghost stories, and have had several of my own personal experiences that led me to believe that there is more to this world than just what we see."

Winn adds, "I began to study ghosts and hauntings from all angles, utilizing websites such as Shadowlands, books, and 'on-the-job' experience. Now as a seasoned paranormal investigator, I have begun to explore deeper into the world of the paranormal and into the science, religious, and psychological aspects of ghosts and hauntings. I have a philosophy that I like to think we can help change the world for the better—one person at a time. I'm involved with a group of people who help others in a way that no one else can. They help people understand why they hear, see, and feel things that others can't. It gives you a very good feeling knowing that you are part of something important."

Steven Carlson: A founding member of LVSSI, Steve also serves as the organization's technical advisor and equipment supervisor. "I am also known as the original LVSSI skeptic. When the other members find something unusual, I do my best to try and find a natural cause for the event before considering the supernatural as an explanation. While I am not always able to attend some of the investigations with the team, I do help Tina analyze both video and photographic evidence collected. I have had a few experiences of my own so I do know that the supernatural exists," he says.

1

The Ghost of Nellis Air Force Base

Location: *Nellis Air Force Base, Nevada*
Paranormal Activity: *Knocking on Doors, Unseen Footsteps, Noises, and EVPs*
Investigators: *Tina and Steven Carlson*

It was during the early 1980s when stories of a haunting at Nellis Air Force Base began to circulate. At that time, reports of ghostly happenings surfaced on the base among the night supervisors, one of which related to the Thunderbird Museum. A gray, shadow-like figure had been seen often in the museum, accompanied by flickering lights and various equipment malfunctions. This gray shadow would appear to linger in the meeting rooms of the hangar, checking on the mechanics and pilots to make sure that they were all doing their jobs and that all was well at the base.

When Tina and Steve Carlson moved to Nellis Air Force Base during the 1990s, Steve worked at this particular building where he began to hear a number of stories about a possible ghost and shared them with Tina. But one ghostly encounter in particular that had caught their attention was of a haunting at a different location on the base and later, when Tina formed the Las Vegas Society of Supernatural Investigations (LVSSI), they decided to check the building out as one of their very first investigations. Many of the night supervisors had personally witnessed a number of ghostly phenomena there that Tina and Steve just couldn't pass up an opportunity to investigate.

As the story goes, one of the military buildings was showing all the signs of a haunting: Footsteps in the hallway, knocking on the doors, and doors unexpectedly slamming shut...all accompanied by a very uncomfortable and uneasy feeling throughout the building. Over a dozen reports of these paranormal occurrences surfaced over time, experienced by numerous night supervisors who were all so terrified of the goings-on that whenever the occurrences would start they would lock themselves in the break room—too scared and shaken to come out and put themselves in the midst of the unknown.

One night in August 2001, Tina and Steve decided to investigate the building for themselves after getting permission from personnel. There would only be one night supervisor working there this particular evening and he made it very clear that he did not want to be part of what the two of them were there for—ghost hunting! After a short time passed, the night supervisor who knew Steve fairly well approached him to let him know that he was going to make an errand to the local store on the base and that he would be back shortly. He also made a point of telling Steve that he would lock the door behind him. Perhaps this was a friendly excuse to make a prompt exit at this point, knowing what lay ahead throughout the course of the long night! This meant that Tina and Steve were now the only two human beings in the building, so they proceeded to set up their equipment, which at that time was fairly limited due to LVSSI being newly formed and this being the preliminary stages of their first investigation.

They placed a tape recording device by the water cooler in the hallway to collect any possible EVPs (Electronic Voice Phenomena), as this was the reported location of the ghostly activity. This device would enable them to capture any unusual spirit voices that would otherwise be inaudible to the human ear. This piece of equipment is now very commonly used among ghost hunters alike and can be extremely successful in capturing voices from the spirit realm. They also placed an EMF (Electromagnetic Field) detector further down in the hallway. A modern day ghost researcher's tracking device, it locates energy sources—both electric and magnetic—and is highly sensitive in detecting fluctuations of the electromagnetic field. Science informs us that we are all created of nothing more than energy and that energy cannot be destroyed; rather, it simply transforms into another type after death.

The psychic medium James Van Praagh describes it best when he uses the example for the transition of human to spirit energy to be similar to that of an ice cube changing from its solid form into a liquid state. Although the ice cube was once solid, its transformation into a liquid form still contains the make-up or source of what it once was—water. As for the spirit energy that was once human form, it will either move on to a higher state of being in the spiritual plane of existence, or it may decide to stay among the living and it is that energy, which remains here on the physical plane, that becomes detectable with such EMF devices. This piece of equipment is therefore extremely important in detecting those unseen lingering energies and it happened to be working positively for Tina and Steve on this particular night—as it was showing signs that there was indeed an unknown presence in the vicinity.

Cameras, of course, were also part of their necessary equipment. They had both a digital and a 35mm camera. Tina immediately started taking photographs, pointing the camera anywhere that she felt an intuitive sense to point it. She took at least two hundred photographs that night that, once developed, revealed an abundance of orb activity; orbs is the term for *spirit balls of light*.

An orb is basically the electromagnetic remnants of a deceased person; a circular shaped ball of spirit energy believed to contain the soul of a person or animal that has departed from the living world. These orbs may sometimes be visible to the naked eye or, as in this case, invisible...until caught on film. They're usually whitish-gray to semi-transparent in color and can appear as any size. Could it perhaps be that the bigger the orb, the more spiritually evolved the person once was?

This night they sat at the opposite ends of the hallway, waiting... which they didn't have to do for very long. Almost immediately the ghost activity began. It was show time!

Suddenly, they heard a suction noise of pressurized air, followed by a loud noise of the front door opening and slamming shut! How could this have been possible, they thought? The night supervisor had definitely locked it behind him. Steve was closest to the door, so he got up to check it. The strangest thing about this was that this particular door had a combination lock to it—no one could possibly have opened it unless they had a numeric code to enter. Not a soul was at the door. This visibly shook Tina and Steve ,who were both excited—and yet alarmed—to see that the activity had already started so strongly. Steve thought that they should think about leaving, but Tina, trying to keep her composure, insisted that they should stay—after all, this was the whole reason why they were there in the first place... Ghost hunting remember?

Tina now went back to sit down at the furthest end of the hallway while Steve decided to stay by the locked door. They could see each other through the darkness; suddenly they heard loud *footsteps* walking down the hallway towards Tina...footsteps of heavy combat boots between the two of them. Steve yelled out to Tina to confirm that what he was hearing were indeed the footsteps. "I hear it too!" Tina yelled back. Tina quickly reminded herself of the reason for them being there, and told herself not to run from the situation and to keep herself grounded.

Suddenly the footsteps came to a halt in the middle of the hallway. Steve shouted to Tina, "Where did they go?" Tina shouted back that she didn't know and for Steve to stay at the end of the hallway just in case the footsteps started to come back his way. She picked up the camera and immediately began taking photographs around the area of where the sound of the ghostly boots had come from. Steve once again shouted out to Tina that he did not feel comfortable being in the building any longer, that they had gathered enough investigative evidence, and should now leave. Tina also began to get the feeling that they were not welcome and that the spirit might become too active—as they were not supposed to be in that area at the time.

Just as Steve was walking down the hallway to meet up with Tina and Tina was walking towards Steve, she happened to pass the water cooler when all of a sudden it started to make a loud clattering noise like that of a fan starting up. She thought this to be really weird and such a coincidence (if it was a coincidence) that it should only now suddenly do this since they had been there for at least a couple of hours and the water cooler had been totally silent the whole time. Steve sometimes worked in the building and was very familiar with the surroundings, but said that this particular water fountain had *never* made such a noise before.

Tina was still finding it hard to accept that it was only now doing this. She kept repeating the question, why should this happen when the footsteps of the boots stopped at precisely that point? After Steve inspected the area of the water cooler with the EMF detector, which showed constant energy fluctuations, he noted the results to be inconclusive; that perhaps the activity was not so paranormal related after all in that area of the hallway due to the close proximity of the electrical wires that were running through

the wall. He again mentioned that, perhaps, whatever it was that was present in the hallway thought that *their* presence was unwarranted and that they should leave. Tina acknowledged his comment that it was indeed time to leave and started to pack up their equipment to go home, where they would then analyze the tapes and all of the other data that they had collected. The night supervisor did eventually return, but Tina and Steve had already left the building, locking the door behind them.

Later that evening, they listened to the tape recording to see if they had captured any EVPs. What they heard on the tape was the sequence of events as they unfolded throughout the night: the door opening and slamming shut, followed by the distinct loud footsteps of the military combat boots walking down the hallway, and Tina asking the question as to why should the water cooler be making this kind of noise now, right where the footsteps ceased. Low and behold in the background of the tape, an unexpected EVP is heard. To their astonishment, they heard a loud guttural male laugh! This laugh was neither interpreted as anything scary or terrifying to them, but on the contrary, that it was more in a playful, joking tone of "I Gotcha" kind of laugh. The ghost had clearly enjoyed a light-hearted moment during the tense situation of the night and had the last laugh...at Tina and Steve's expense!

Conclusion

Even though this investigation was the very first for LVSSI, which only consisted of two members back then, the team did collect results of paranormal activity in the building. The EMF detector showed erratic electromagnetic fluctuations in certain areas of the hallway that night, which showed that an active energy was present...something that was other than human. However, by the water cooler, the EMF detector responded to a normal energy source—electrical wires running through the wall—and unrelated to any paranormal activity. Spirit orbs were also captured with their cameras, as well as the ghostly footsteps heard on the recording and the unexpected EVP of a male voice laughing that was inaudible at the time of their investigation.

Unfortunately they could not perform a cleansing at this location, as this would have required an open flame from burning sage and would be against the fire-safety rules of the base, especially since open flames cannot be used in any Government building without prior authorization. To this day it's reported that ghostly activity still continues at Nellis Air Force Base—and the night supervisors still *hide* out in the break room whenever they hear the footsteps of those mysterious ghostly combat boots walking down the hallway!

I see you
Beware

2

Writing On the Mirrors

Location: *Summerlin, Las Vegas Nevada*
Paranormal Activity: *Moving of Objects, Voices, Writing on the Mirrors, and Electrical Disturbances*
Investigators: *Tina and Steve Carlson, Nancy Riggs, Matthew Winn, and LVSSI Trainees*

Some hauntings are more intense than others, and this next investigation turns out to be one of those cases. This ghost had every intention of letting itself be heard, seen, and felt, and would do everything it possibly could to remain in the family's home.

David Robertson is a very successful businessman, and in May of 2005 he wrote a lengthy email to LVSSI stating that he, his wife, and son had recently moved into their home in the Summerlin area of Nevada and were extremely disturbed about a number of possible ghostly occurrences that were taking place there. At first, they were very happy and excited to move into their beautiful dream home, but they quickly became very worried and concerned...as they did not expect to be sharing their house with a resident ghost!

A myriad of ghostly happenings were going on and had initially taken place over a nine-month period; it had gotten so that David and his family had decided that enough was enough! They contacted LVSSI to see if they could help. In his email, he listed all of the occurrences that the family had witnessed to date. For some reason, this ghost liked to switch on all of the televisions throughout the house, no particular channel, but just that of a snowy white screen. The gas fireplaces would all be turned on randomly. Lights, ceiling fans, and bathroom fans were also being tampered with.

Although all of these experiences were disrupting enough, David went on to say that the paranormal activity had become much worse. *This ghost* decided to take the much bolder step of *communicating* with his family by writing messages on the mirror and the glass shower door in their master bathroom. These messages were not happy ones—and were very direct. This really bothered the family considerably, especially David's wife, as she was the one who always seemed to find them. There had been five written messages over the course of nine months: *BEWARE*, *LEAV* (missing the E at the end,) *BOO*, *I SEE YOU*, and *MINE*. David also told the team that he had decided to keep a journal noting all of the detailed activities as and when they occurred, especially as they increased.

He added that the room where most of the activity happened was in the guest bedroom, where the family kept several antiques. Let me point out here that keeping antiques in your home is not always a good thing to do, as it can attract unwanted visitors in your space. That is, of course, if the antiques have not been fully cleansed beforehand. Although these objects can be a prized collector's item and hold high value, let's not forget that they can often be extremely old and carry a certain amount of history attached to them. How many times has an item circulated from family to family? Perhaps it was once in the possession of a person who died and their spirit did not want to give up this much-loved antique. Could this have been the case here with the Robertson family? Another added point to the email was that, they noticed in the guest bedroom that there was often a strong odor that smelled like urine, but seemed to vanish once the activity subsided.

Mr. Robertson went on to say in his email, "I've never believed in the supernatural, but I'm now starting to believe something definitely does exist." He wanted to set up a meeting with the team to discuss the activity in more detail. LVSSI investigator Matthew Winn replied to his email and they immediately arranged to meet.

The Robertsons' home was an extremely beautiful large house with fourteen rooms, approximately ten-years-old, and was once owned by the Howard Hughes Corporation with no prior reports of any such ghostly activity. When the team arrived at the house, Steve began setting up much of their equipment, which included the EVP machine, the EMF devices, and their cameras. Tina began by sitting down with Mr. Robertson and his wife as they described the ghostly happenings in more detail. Throughout the night's long investigation, the homeowners were invited to accompany the team as they investigated the various rooms in their house. Tina was the main investigator and she would also be assisting the trainees in how to use the investigative equipment, tending to their needs, and answering any questions that arose regarding the paranormal occurrences.

David and his wife described to Tina how they had every so often been hearing the distinct mumbling sound of a male voice. They would also prepare their house bills at the counter in the kitchen, only to have them disappear and then reappear at the end of the counter, and the ghost would then put them underneath a place mat. They went on to say that the French doors leading onto the balcony of their master bedroom were routinely opened and left wide open throughout the entire day, but said they remembered checking that all of the doors were definitely locked before leaving the house on any given day.

They also recalled the morning they walked into the kitchen and saw, to their astonishment, all of the cupboard doors were wide open and all of the kitchen drawers were pulled out! There were always repeated problems with the electrical devices such as the ceiling fan in the guest bedroom that periodically switched on and off, and closet lights being turned on all by themselves. At first David and his wife thought that all of the activity could be explained and that, perhaps, they were accidentally causing it...*until* the writing started to appear on the mirror and the shower doors in the bathroom. LVSSI witnessed this for themselves during their investigation, amazed to see the word "*BEWARE*" actually *being written* on the shower glass door. They described the writing to be like that of a wax crayon to the touch, or resembling that of a smear from a finger when the glass steams up. This writing had no color to it and was clear, and even touching it felt strange.

They described the letters of the writing to be very distinctive, an old English type of writing style from the 1700s, with lots of scrolls and curls to the letters. The team immediately started taking photographs of the message, but unfortunately when the photographs were later developed, they did not turn out too clearly due to the reflection from the camera flash in the glass. I would like to mention here that LVSSI always acts as their own skeptics at all times when analyzing their photographic evidence. They always make sure that what they have collected is genuine paranormal phenomena before showing them to anyone and certainly before featuring them on their website. They will very often disregard any questionable photographs that they believe people will be skeptical of or unsure about. As professional investigators, they will only put forward photographic evidence that cannot be mistaken or misidentified for anything other than true paranormal phenomena.

The team decided to wipe off the writing from the mirrored surfaces, but shortly after doing so they were shocked to discover that the ghost had mischievously removed the bathroom doorstop from behind the door! They continued walking through the house to investigate things further, and found that doors that had been open were now closed and doors that had been closed were now open. It appeared that this spirit would not let up and was using every opportunity it had of showing its presence. It was during this two-hour investigation that yet another message was written on the same shower glass door, but it now read "*LEAV*" with the *E* missing at the end. The team felt that it was a direct message to them...that this ghost was annoyed at their presence and wanted them immediately out of the house!

Nancy happened to be checking out the downstairs family room at the time when she noticed a strange and intense smell in there. It resembled that of a lacquer or a varnish type smell, which she immediately attributed to a possible re-varnishing of a piece of the family's furniture. But since this was not the case, she was at a loss to find out what the smell actually was and where it was coming from. She also felt a burning sensation in her throat that made it very difficult for her to breathe, as well as a feeling of getting warmer and extremely dizzy. Nancy knew that she immediately needed to get out of there and made her way to the foyer of the house, where Matthew was standing and was about to investigate the dining room area. They both explained to each other how they had previously been drawn to this particular part of the house and that it happened to be one of the locations where the fireplace was always being mysteriously switched on and off. As Steve was now standing on the landing, Matthew was in the dining room and immediately shouted out. "There's someone down there!" Matthew and Nancy both witnessed the outline of the shadow of a man, but they could not make out any details of clothing or facial features. There was just the dark shadow.

Matthew pointed the camera to the exact area where the mysterious figure was seen, snapping as many photos as he could. Later, once the photographs had been developed, he noticed that one of them revealed a spirit orb as clear as day. As they investigated various areas of the house that night, the EMF devices fluctuated quite considerably from room to room, showing that there was a definite change in the magnetic and electrical fields of the environment. In other words, the devices were being activated by the unseen presence around the house.

Nancy recalled another strange experience while she and a trainee were checking out the master bedroom closet. As they sat on the floor of the closet area, Nancy noticed a glow around the trainee's face. It was quite dark in the closet, so the glow was fairly prominent. At this point, she asked the trainee, "Do you feel anything unusual?"

"Yes," answered the trainee, "I feel like my face is being cupped by a pair of hands."

Nancy was totally taken aback by her reply, and described to her what she had just seen.

There were a number of experiences that Nancy played witness to during the night's investigation. While in one of the bathrooms, she heard someone breathing behind her... followed by a cold sensation filling the room...followed by a loud thump! This obviously caught Nancy's attention and she looked around the room to see where it could possibly be coming from. She even checked the air conditioning and bathroom fan, making sure they were switched off, and that there were no windows open. Once again there was *no* explanation for these strange occurrences...yet it was apparent that an unknown presence was definitely keeping Nancy company!

The next room that they investigated was the study. All of the team experienced a very strange sensation in here as though the floor was somewhat tilted. The room also had a strong, sweet bubble gum smell. They had no idea where it could possibly have come from, and checked every part of the room to see if there was some explanation for it, but, again, they found nothing. As they had now reached the end of their investigation at the Robertson home, LVSSI decided to fully cleanse the property and rid the ghost from their home once and for all.

A series of sacred prayers were spoken by the team, followed by the burning of ancient herbs sage and sweet grass. They also used sea salt, which was placed around all openings of doors and windows. They went room to room—thoroughly performing their cleansing ritual—until every space had been cleansed. Their work was done.

In this one and the other investigations they perform, LVSSI usually recite two prayers, an opening prayer and a closing prayer. During this time, they stand, close their eyes, and bow their heads. Quite often after saying a prayer, they feel that the ghost or spirit has immediately left, as they *feel* the house becoming much quieter than when they first arrived. *(Author's note: For your information, the prayers recited by LVSSI are listed in the back of the book.)*

The Robertsons called LVSSI after a week had passed to let them know that the cleansing had made an immediate, positive impact in their home. They were extremely grateful to the team for all of their efforts, which had brought normalcy back into their home. But a couple of weeks later, the Robertsons contacted the team again, horrified to see yet another written message appear on their bathroom mirror. This time the ghost wrote two words—*NO GOD*. Each letter was written extremely long in length...as if the spirit was trying to over state the message to the family.

The team immediately headed back to the house and repeated the cleansing ritual for a second time, performing it with much more intensity to eliminate all of the negative energies that were still dwelling there. The second cleansing appeared to be a success! To everyone's delight, the ghost finally decided to move on, and all was now peaceful once more at the Robertson family residence.

Conclusion

In most cases a spirit cleansing is only needed to be performed once for it to be successful. However, this situation was a little different as the haunting at this home was a fairly intense one, to say the least. All of the electronic devices used during this investigation showed that there was, indeed a powerful and unseen presence in the Robertsons' home. From the collection of photographs that LVSSI had taken, one photograph actually captured the image of a spirit orb in the exact location where the shadow figure was seen.

The EMF Meter actively showed electromagnetic fluctuations throughout the many rooms in the house—once again showing undeniable proof to LVSSI and the family that the unseen was undoubtedly being detected.

Also, upon reviewing the EVP recordings, the team heard a distinct male voice speaking three times at different points on the tape. These voices were not heard at the time of the investigation, however.

★ The first EVP said: "I scare the brother."

★ The second EVP begins with the investigator asking a team member, "With the flashlight on or off?" Tina's voice is then heard replying, "Off," to which the spirit voice says, "I know."

★ The third EVP begins fairly quiet after a few words were spoken by the team...and then the spirit voice clearly says, "This is *my* house."

All EVP recordings were thoroughly analyzed through an appropriate and reliable audio analysis source at the time, to which LVSSI learned that this unknown voice was definitely not the voice of any human being.

KESARA

3

Grandpa Waiting

Location: *Sunrise Mountain Area, Las Vegas, Nevada*
Paranormal Activity: *Voices, Noises, Whispering, and Seeing Shadows*
Investigators: *Nancy Riggs, Tina and Steve Carlson, Matthew Winn, and LVSSI Trainees*

This ghostly encounter is one of the more friendly kind. HE tried to communicate with the couple on a regular basis, and although they didn't believe it to be friendly at first, it was only with the help of LVSSI and the use of the dowsing rods that the spirit relayed a positive message to the couple of who he was and why he was present in their home.

LVSSI member Nancy Riggs was approached one day by one of her work colleagues, Peter Dunn, who happened to know of her involvement with the organization and their passion for ghost hunting. Peter asked Nancy if she and the team could help solve the reoccurring paranormal activity that he and his wife Denise appeared to be experiencing at their home.

The Dunns were a fairly young couple in their mid thirties and had lived at their house for only two years. They also had three pets; two dogs and a cat. Within six months of moving into their home, they both started sensing—and witnessing—some very peculiar things. At first, they totally dismissed it; Denise especially thinking, more often than not, it was her husband playing jokes on her, or that they both had overactive imaginations and their minds were playing tricks on them.

Peter would frequently hear his name being called and would see odd black shapes out of the corner of his eye. He was the first to notice this strange activity, but it would not be too long before Denise would also catch sight of these odd black shapes and shadows moving around various parts of the home. The pets were also becoming very disturbed by these occurrences, behaving strangely whenever they sensed the paranormal invading their space. Whatever it was, they were scared by it.

One day, while playing with his two dogs inside the house, Peter's attention was pulled to the ceiling. The ceiling fan chains were swinging erratically back and forth, and as he looked up towards the high ceiling and saw this, he wondered what in the world could be causing it, as there appeared to be no apparent explanation for it. There was no airflow from any air vent, nor were any windows open. There was no air circulation from any source whatsoever. His wife had also occasionally noticed the fan chains swinging back and forth, but she immediately dismissed it and thought it to be Peter playing a joke on her.

All of this bizarre activity started to repeat itself most evenings around the time of 7 p.m., and the bewildered couple then started to question whether it was indeed a supernatural force at work. It was at this point that they called Nancy and the team in to investigate things further.

LVSSI arrived at the house with a few of their investigative trainees one evening, and the couple described all that they had experienced over the past few months. The dogs were placed in a different room so that they would not bother the team as they explored the house. Tina decided to sit in the dining room area to see if any paranormal activity would show itself, and as she sat there mentally tuning herself into the surroundings, within moments she caught sight of a small spirit orb—that manifested into a larger one—slowly moving across one of the dining room walls. She then watched as it retraced its movement, continuing to float across the wall and then...disappear.

At this point she realized that the EMF meters were with the rest of the team, as were the cameras and other pieces of equipment, and so she did not have the opportunity of capturing the phenomena on any one of the devices. She also witnessed other strange light activity throughout the house that night—and a dark shadow looming around in the guitar room. There was also a hand bell in there that Peter said on occasions would mysteriously ring all by itself.

As Nancy walked around the home, she was pulled towards what she called the 'cat room,' which happened to be a fairly small room where the cat's litter box was kept. She felt a sudden dizziness in here and a very strong sensation that *someone* (or some thing) was with her, but of course nothing was visible to the naked eye... except for a strange light a couple of inches in size. She saw it appear—and quickly disappear—from sight. Was this another spirit orb phenomena?

The team also experienced problems with their walkie-talkies and found it difficult to communicate with one another from room-to-room. It appeared that some unseen force was intervening and stopping them from messaging back and forth. Nancy conferred with Tina that maybe she ought to try and communicate with whoever *it* was...as the spirit clearly wanted to be noticed. As Peter and Denise stood watching nearby, she picked up the metal dowsing rods and began preparing herself for asking a series of questions to the resident spirit. She had an immediate feeling that this was a family member, but couldn't decipher if it was belonging to Peter or Denise...yet she distinctly heard the word "Poppi" in her head.

Tina, who was in the hallway, said that she had also felt it to be a family member and said that he's waiting for something—and watching. She had received very strong impressions that this was a grandfather figure watching over the couple as their guardian—and that he strongly wanted them to have a baby—and that *he would stay* for as long it took for this to happen. Funnily enough, Peter and Denise conveyed to Nancy and Tina that they had in fact been planning to have a baby for some time, but as of that time had not been successful.

Nancy began to direct her questions to the Grandpa. If his answers were positive, the rods would cross over each other; if they were negative, they would swing apart.

Nancy: "Are you hear to watch over them?"
Grandpa: *"Yes."*
Nancy: "Are you waiting for a grandchild?"
Grandpa: *"Yes."*
Nancy: "Do you like the pets?"

To this, Grandpa replied, "Yes," but he also transmitted thoughts to Nancy of how he found the cat to have too much energy. The Grandpa added that he liked the house and in particular the bedroom that they were standing in, which he considered to be perfect for a grandchild. It was now starting to dawn on Denise that it was indeed her grandfather, and neither she nor Peter wanted him to leave. They knew that he meant them no harm...that his presence in the home was one of a benevolent nature and of a guardian figure to watch over them and take care of them...and to be there especially to see a grandchild welcomed into the world.

Tina suggested that Peter and Denise should acknowledge Grandpa's presence and let him know that they were aware of his good intentions towards them—even though his paranormal antics had scared them to no end—and let him know that they didn't mind him staying in their home as long as he stopped scaring them with his *supernatural* antics.

The team respected the wishes of Denise and Peter—they really wanted the Grandpa to stay—and did not proceed with a house cleansing that night. This procedure is usually the final part of any investigation that the team becomes involved with, but only at the homeowner's request. The couple was now left knowing that the presence of this spirit was indeed a happy and benevolent one, and that his intentions were only good ones. All was now becoming peaceful at the couple's home...well, at least for a little while.

After a month had passed, Nancy and the team were called back to the house as the paranormal activity was now intensifying. Although the couple had done exactly what Tina suggested they do and acknowledge the Grandfather's presence, the activity wasn't stopping or slowing down. It seemed that the more attention they gave him, the more he would act up. Peter had become so frustrated with the situation that he couldn't help but to now shout and yell at him, becoming much more aggressive in his tone, which did not help matters at all.

Tina advised Peter that he must stop shouting at the spirit as it would only antagonize him more. Instead, she said, he should act more respectful to him...just as if he was there in physical form. Peter admitted that he thought this would be difficult to do, but he would at least try his best and respect Grandpa as much as possible. Peter kept to his word—and that helped foster a better relationship between him and the Spirit Grandpa.

Whenever Nancy now sees Peter at work, she asks how things are going at home with Grandpa.

"Oh he's at it again," Peter said. "I just have to remember to be respectful and tell him to stop it. That if he is going to be mischievous and do something paranormal, to please alert us and do it during the daytime and not at night when we are trying to get some sleep!"

Conclusion

The conclusion to this investigation was truly a happy one, and at the time of writing this chapter, Denise and Peter were expecting their first child in May 2008. They have conveyed the baby news to Grandpa, but chances are he already knew. Initially Denise experienced a few problems at the beginning of her pregnancy, as she had been diagnosed with an ectopic one, and she and Peter had originally planned to have the pregnancy terminated when they heard the not-so-good news. However, as soon as she had scheduled the procedure to terminate the fetus—call it divine intervention—but the fetus then started to locate itself to where it was able to fully develop, and Denise and Peter are very excited to be bringing their first child into the world. Was this a little divine intervention from Grandpa? One can only imagine, and smile!

4

The Hanging Barbie Doll

Location: *South Las Vegas, Nevada*
Paranormal Activity: *Moving of Objects, Whispering, and Dark Shadows*
Investigators: *Tina and Steve Carlson, Nancy Riggs, Matthew Winn, and two trainees*

Louise was a young mother of two small girls ages six and nine who became increasingly alarmed for her daughters' well being, when a whole manner of paranormal manifestations started to occur in their home and on a frequent basis. It was a new house that comfortably suited her family's needs, and after moving in, the first couple of months were very exciting—as moving into any new house often is—until of course the paranormal began showing signs of its presence.

After seeing an article in a local newspaper about LVSSI and their successful ghost-busting work, Louise decided to make contact with the team and invite them to investigate her home, as the activity had now become too overwhelming. Of course, like most people, Louise did not believe in ghosts *until* she was confronted with the phenomena herself, but as her children had been experiencing some very odd things, her concern for them was growing daily. At first, Louise did not connect the goings-on with a ghost. Instead, she thought that it was someone trying to break into the house, but the activity was happening too frequently—at least three times a week!—for that to be the case.

She and her children were not the only ones to witness the myriad of ghostly encounters; her boyfriend had also experienced a culmination of strange things and had become really terrified by it all. He was also becoming concerned for Louise, who was now becoming increasingly anxious over the whole situation. They had also rented out a downstairs room in the home to someone who would help with the house costs and regularly babysit the children when they needed him to. But, as it turned out, it was only within a short period of time that he too would witness the strange encounters in the home. This would scare him so much that he would very often stay at his girlfriend's house, only to eventually move out of Louise's home completely. Though the paranormal was something he did not believe in, he couldn't cope with it any longer and didn't want to put himself in the middle of a haunting.

There had been countless knocking sounds, whispering, objects being moved around the house, and problems with electrical devices such as lights and televisions being switched on and off periodically. The doorbell would ring all by itself, and the garage door would routinely open and close. Most of these occurrences happened around the time of midnight, making it impossible for the family to sleep. Just as they would settle down for the night...the activity would start.

LVSSI met with Louise and her boyfriend for a preliminary meeting one evening, which they followed with a complete house investigation a week later. Louise thought it best for her children to be out of the house that night and took them to stay at her mother's home. Little did the team know upon arriving that the investigation would take a whole three hours, and throughout the entire evening, every single one of them would sense the presence of the paranormal in one manner or another. Tina started the investigation by sitting with the couple to talk about all of the strange events that had been unfolding over the past five months, then the team separated to explore each and every room.

As they began to make their way around the various rooms, Matthew decided to make his way upstairs to the master bedroom. In one of the corners of the room was a tall plant, a palm tree, and to his astonishment, what he saw manifesting was quite disturbing. Within minutes of being in the room, he witnessed the *face of a man floating across the wall*...only to embed itself behind the palm tree and *stare out* at Matthew! As it happened, one of the EMF meters that had been placed in the room at the time started to erratically light up—a sure sign that this bodiless entity was, indeed, present.

Some of the other investigators had also later made their way upstairs to check out the rooms. While coming back down the stairs, Steve immediately felt as though someone was pushing him from behind. All of a sudden he would throw out his arms to catch his balance by holding on to the walls, his feet spread apart as they slid down every stair with such force. Although shocked and surprised by this, Steve, being the skeptical one of the team, just dismissed it as simply losing his balance and continued walking down the stairs as if nothing had happened. But the rest of the team had witnessed the sheer force of the push and were adamant that some unseen force had definitely pushed him.

Another occurrence that they experienced was the disturbances of their walkie-talkies. It was as if something was pushing the button to talk, but no voices were heard coming through. Because this happened so often throughout the investigation, they decided to change the frequency of them, but once changed over they still kept showing signs of interference.

In the downstairs area of the house was another bedroom that was partly empty all but for a small mattress and some clutter. As they entered this room, a small alarm clock suddenly sounded very loudly, scaring everyone to no end. But while in the room, Tina kept being drawn to the closet area and shouted out to the others.

"Hey, there's something going on in here!" she said.

Dark shadows were moving around in the closet, causing quite a stir. Nancy had also noticed an orb on the wall by the closet—a fair sized orb that they felt coincided with the activity Tina was witnessing. Nancy picked up her 35mm camera and immediately started taking photographs of it.

Nancy often had some quiet time by herself during many of the investigations, and while in one of the rooms in this house, she felt a very odd sensation of melting into the floor. This was a unique experience for Nancy—she had never felt anything like it in any of the other investigations—and at the time of it happening she had no idea that this was a sensation being passed on to her by a spirit that was trying to contact her. It would be many months later during other investigations that this sensation of melting into the floor would repeat itself numerous times and, only in retrospect, did she realize that it was indeed a spirit trying to communicate with her.

Next door to this room was the children's bedroom, where the team and the owners got the biggest shock of their lives! They had been in this particular bedroom previously that night to investigate it, but nothing was out of place. Yet, when they all decided to go back into the bedroom for another look, there hanging from the ceiling was...one of the children's Barbie Dolls hanging by her hair! This obviously happened when everyone left the room after their initial investigation; after all, they had been together at all times, including Louise and her boyfriend, so it would have been impossible for anyone to have gone back to the room and arranged this as some kind of a practical joke.

They all stood there, looked at each other in

stunned disbelief. How could this have happened? They just couldn't believe what their eyes were seeing. After a few minutes passed, sounds of laughter gradually started to fill the room. Then they all knew it was the spirit trying to communicate with them and letting them know of its definite presence. They started taking photographs of the hanging Barbie Doll. They all agreed that they wished they could have witnessed the doll floating up towards the ceiling in mid-air and to have captured the whole event on camera!

During the final hour of the investigation, the team performed their usual house cleansing ritual of burning the herbs sage and sweet grass while going room-to-room, speaking their prayers of protection as they did. Salt was placed around every doorframe and along the windowsills, as well as all entrances to the house. Salt is a purifier, a natural earth element that is very useful in warding off negativity and any unwanted spirits.

Within a few days after the investigation, the team received a wonderful thank you letter from Louise and her boyfriend, letting them know that the house was now clean and free of the paranormal occurrences. They were happy to know that at last they could settle in their new home without the concerns of an unwanted spirit guest!

Conclusion

Although this home had some very strong paranormal activity, only one cleansing was needed to remove the unwanted spirit from this residence. Among the plethora of occurrences, the strangest of all was the hanging Barbie Doll. While the team and the homeowners were initially shocked at seeing this, they knew that it was a deliberate attempt on the part of the spirit to get their attention and to let them know it was present in their home. It just goes to prove that spirits will go to any lengths to capture your attention—no matter what it takes.

Although it was not possible for LVSSI to actually film this paranormal event in action, other photographs did reveal two orbs by the closet area in the babysitter's bedroom. No EVPs were recorded that night, and photographs from this investigation can be seen at the teams' website.

KESARA

5

Korean Doll

Location: *Nellis Air Force Base, Nevada*
Paranormal Activity: *Voices, Moving of Objects, and Orb Activity*
Investigators: *Tina and Steve Carlson*

What would you do if a ghost repeatedly moved an object to get your attention, and no matter how many times you put the object back, the ghost continuously keeps placing it in the same spot? Every so often you might hear of a ghost story where the spirit has an attachment to an object and finds it difficult to separate itself... as this ghost investigation shows.

The Jenson family were a traditional American family of four living on the Nellis Air Force Base; Tom, his wife Kim, and their two young children, ages seven and nine. It was during the month of November 2001 that Tom happened to read an article in a local Las Vegas newspaper about Tina and her husband's work with Shadowlands Ghost Investigations, another successful paranormal team that Tina had been involved with for a number of years prior to forming her own investigations group, LVSSI.

Tom and his family had been experiencing ghostly phenomena for a number of months since moving onto the base, and after reading of LVSSI's work in successfully removing unwanted spirits, Tom decided to contact Tina to ask that she and her husband Steve come to investigate their home. He and his wife were constantly hearing voices and objects were being moved around the house. Tom had experienced prior ghost activity some years ago and, as a result of it, did actually believe in the supernatural, but this situation was now causing him to become concerned for his family. Of course Tina was eager to try and help the family, and immediately set up an appointment to visit with the Jensons at their home.

At first Tom thought there would be a problem with LVSSI's visit due to his family living on an Air Force Base; as it had only been a couple of months since the terrible 9/11 tragedy, it might be somewhat difficult for them to be allowed a pass onto the base, especially since the horrific event had resulted in security measures being strictly reinforced at all Government locations. However, Tom was unaware that Tina and Steve also lived at the same base, and once Tina explained this to him, there was no longer an issue. As it turned out, Tom and his family only lived a short distance away from Tina and Steven, and upon a preliminary meeting taking place, Tom quickly realized that he and Steve in fact knew each other from working at various parts of the base. That made the initial visit very comfortable, with Tom feeling that Tina and Steve were very trustworthy.

Tina sat with Kim in the living room and took notes of all of the paranormal goings-on that had happened while Tom showed Steve various areas in the dining room where they have been hearing strange noises. Kim began to describe every detail of the repeated ghostly interference that they were *all* experiencing, including their two young children; the kids were now even afraid to walk down the hallway that leads to their bedrooms because they would often hear footsteps and whispers there. They also have been awakened every night by various noises.

There were always certain disturbances coming from the kitchen; the sound of plates clattering and dishes rattling in the cupboards on their own accord, not to mention a female voice calling out: "Kim, are you there? Kim?" But the most alarming of all was the fact that *every evening* Kim would find her special childhood Korean Doll placed right in the middle of the living room floor! This doll was an ornamental doll and fairly fancy—the type of doll that would usually be placed in an ideal part of the room for everyone to admire. It had been a gift to Kim from her Great-Grandmother when she was just a little girl, and Kim always kept the doll in her hope chest in one of the bedrooms.

As Tina started to put pen to paper, taking notes of what had been happening, she started to get a very strong feeling that someone was watching them, and no matter how much she tried to keep her focus on the note taking, she found it very difficult. Kim could see that Tina was obviously becoming somewhat distracted by something and asked her what exactly she was sensing. "I feel that there's a lady here, an older lady," Tina said. Kim asked if she could to describe the spirit to her.

"This lady is not much taller than 4'5"," Tina said. "She's very, very short in stature and I get the feeling that she had a medical condition of either Scoliosis or Osteoporosis, as I see her hunched over somewhat and walking with her head down. It's not too clear at the moment," Tina continued, "but she's very polite and liked to laugh a lot and I can tell you that she's right here with us."

Kim acknowledged the information that Tina was relaying to her, nodding her head in agreement. "The lady you are describing is my Great-Grandmother," Kim said, "and the doll that appears in the middle of the floor was a gift from her when I was a child." Kim's Great-Grandmother had told her as a little girl that as long as she kept the doll she would always be with her.

Kim became very emotional and could no longer hold back her tears as Tina described with accuracy her great-grandmother, remembering the childhood connection to her and the memories of being given this beautiful Korean doll.

"It's okay," Tina said. "She's letting you know that there's no reason to cry and that she loves you very much and wants to let you know that she's always around you."

While Kim appreciated the validity of knowing that her Great-Grandmother was always present, she wasn't too happy with how her grandmother's communication was disturbing the children and asked Tina to pass the message on to her.

"She's right here," said Tina. "Just talk to her as if she was physically here because she would much prefer to hear the message from you than from me."

Kim realized that what Tina was saying made sense and took the bold step of communicating with her Grandmother, who was on the *other side*.

"Grandma," she said, "I love you and I've always loved you. I am really happy that you're here watching over me and my family, but could you please keep your actions and your communication limited to just myself and Tom because the children don't understand and they're scared to hear and see what you're doing? I don't care what type of actions you display towards me and Tom; the voices, or what kind of things you do and show us, but please leave the children alone."

Tina quickly interrupted and said that she could see Kim's Grandmother standing there and that she was saying, "Yes, okay, I'll do that for you, I can do that." She acknowledged everything Kim asked of her. But it was only on one condition that her Grandmother would keep her word, relaying her own message that she wanted to pass on to Kim: Kim had to keep the doll out of the hope chest at all times because if it was hidden away, Kim would not be giving her Grandmother the acknowledgement that she needed. She also desperately wanted Kim to know that she was present at all times. So with that, Kim said that she would keep the doll out of the hope chest and in more of a public view. She kept her promise and sure enough the doll was no longer moved and stayed in the place where Kim had put her. Although this immediately seemed to solve the problem, from time to time Kim would still hear her Grandmother's voice shouting out her name, "Kim! Kim!"

Several months had passed, and the Jenson family made the decision to relocate to a different Air Force Base. They packed up all of their belongings in preparation of the move and looked forward to a new home and new surroundings. When they did finally arrive at their new residence, it would be many days before any of their belongings were unpacked. Not a single item was taken out of the piles of boxes. During their very first night of moving into their new home, low and behold, there was the Korean doll sitting in the middle of the living room floor! The message was very loud and clear to Kim—that once again she was to put the doll on display at all times—and keep her Grandmother's presence in the home always.

Conclusion

Sometimes when the spirit of a relative or a loved one comes to visit, the family often feels that they don't want them to leave, and in a strange kind of way they feel quite honored that spirit should pay them a visit, once they know that the spirit is indeed a family member.

As this was the case with the Jenson family, no house cleansing was carried out to enable the Great Grandmother to move on, and once Kim had acknowledged the fact that the doll was to be kept out of the hope chest at all times, it seemed to solve the problem of the paranormal activity reoccurring. Although LVSSI did not capture any EVPs from this investigation, they did take a number of photographs, which showed signs of a very strange mist, and a collection of spirit orbs. Throughout the investigation, it took only two visits to the family's home to solve the problems of the haunting.

KESARA

6

Candles on the Stairs

Location: *North Las Vegas, Nevada*
Paranormal Activity: *Candles being placed on the stairs, Voices, Moving of Objects, and Disturbances*
Investigators: *Nancy Riggs, Tina and Steve Carlson, Matthew Winn, and LVSSI Trainees*

How would you react if you distinctly heard the voice of a ghost telling you that it was going to take a nap? Would you howl with laughter? Try to ignore it? Think that it's tiring work being a ghost, or that you were going slightly mad? If the answer was yes to all four of these questions, congratulations! These were the same thoughts and reactions of the couple in this next ghost investigation, as this is precisely what Ellen and her husband Tim heard in their home one day in May 2005. In fact they would constantly hear a couple of distinct male voices trying to communicate with them at various times throughout the day and night...one of which would repeatedly tell Ellen that he was in love with her!

The house that Ellen and Tim had purchased was brand new and situated in the Lone Mountain area of North Las Vegas. They had barely lived there less than a year when paranormal occurrences started to unfold, and after the couple read an article about LVSSI in a local Nevada newspaper, they immediately contacted the team about helping them with their paranormal disturbances. LVSSI agreed to take on this new investigation. The house was so new that at first it was difficult for the team members to actually locate it due to the mass construction work in the developing area, but once the team located the property they were eager to meet the family and begin their ghost investigation.

The couple had three children, a ten-year-old and four-year-old twins, and while the kids apparently were not experiencing any of the paranormal activity that Ellen and Tim were, as parents they were naturally concerned and extremely anxious for their children's safety. The family pets, however, were always scared of something, and would react in a very frightened, alarming way when they sensed the unknown presence intruding the house. For example, their pet ferret would often become very agitated at an unseen presence and would snap and bite at the family for no apparent reason, which, according to Ellen, was a sure sign to her that something paranormal was about to happen as he would never usually behave in this way. The dogs and the cat would also sense strange things in various parts of the house, and quite often the cat's litter box would be repeatedly moved and knocked around in the laundry room, even when none of the other animals were in that part of the house.

As Tina would always be the investigator to initially sit with the owners and talk with them about their paranormal situation—and help put their fears at ease—the other investigators would choose various rooms in the house to explore. Usually, these were rooms that they felt drawn to, often times sensing a certain energy in them. Ellen began explaining to Tina in more detail how she and Tim were constantly hearing male voices and that there were certain hot and cold spots in various parts of the house. Objects would frequently be moved, and the hot water in the shower would always be so cold that they would have to turn it to a much higher level in order to compensate. In particular, the ghost—or ghosts—would repeatedly move miscellaneous religious candles, always placing them on the stairs!

This would really bother the family since the candles were kept nowhere near the staircase; they were usually sitting on the counter in the kitchen. When LVSSI asked the family about this bizarre behavior, they were at a loss to explain why this should happen. They also said that there was no significance to the staircase at all. The family's faith was that of non-denominational Christians; it was anybody's (wild) guess if this could somehow be the reason or possible connection to the moving of the candles, or whether the spirit's faith was once the opposite of theirs and maybe the spirit was trying to challenge their religion in some way. They just didn't have any idea as to what the ghost were trying to express by doing this.

Besides their other pets, they also had a fish tank that was kept in the living room. The family noticed that strange things would occur on a regular basis to this tank, as the water level would mysteriously keep decreasing, and they would have to re-fill it repeatedly in such a short space of time to maintain its normal water level. But there was another weird occurrence that was happening that the family knew there had to be a connection to. They would frequently find puddles of water that would appear from nowhere upstairs in one of the bedrooms, and as they would find these water puddles, the fish tanks water level would always be getting lower. They definitely felt there was a correlation between the two because they would never find just one of the occurrences happening without the other. There was just no sense to this ghostly behavior, but as we find in so many hauntings, paranormal activity seldom makes little sense anyway.

While Tina was gathering information from the homeowners, the other team members were spread out in the house. Nancy experienced a rather scary incident on the stairs...the same stairs where the ghost was placing the religious candles.

"Whoa, somebody help me!" she said. "I feel like someone's trying to push me over the edge!"

It was such an intense feeling and the push so forceful that other members of the team had to intervene and tightly hold on to

her while she grabbed onto the walls to regain her balance. She felt such an ominous feeling throughout the whole experience, and once she was able to, she quickly walked down the stairs and went into a different part of the house to sit and get back to feeling like her usual self again.

The team had taken a few trainees with them on this investigation, and one man in particular was an expert in the field of dowsing. This man played an important and significant role in LVSSI, as he taught the members how to locate unseen energies and lay lines with the use of the dowsing rods. On this evening, he had brought along a pendulum and was looking for various objects in the house to dowse. He discovered a poster in one of the children's bedrooms of the cartoon character Buzz Lightyear and took it off the wall to see what would happen if he used the pendulum over it. The pendulum went absolutely crazy, rapidly swinging backwards and forwards all over the poster. He watched in utter amazement, and sat there for a whole hour with this poster trying to fathom why it was happening. After all, according to what Ellen and Tim had told Tina, their three children had never experienced any of the paranormal occurrences nor had they ever witnessed anything out of the ordinary, so it was strange to see the pendulum reacting over this poster that belonged to one of the children and had been hanging in their bedroom. The only explanation that he and the team could come up with was that perhaps this poster had been picked up at a yard sale and the energy of a previous owner was still hanging on to it.

The haunting, though, wasn't only happening inside the home, but also outside. In fact, neighboring properties were also being affected. The house next door to Ellen's was also newly-built and vacant, yet Ellen and Tim explained how most evenings a light would suddenly come on all by itself—even though the house was empty. So the team decided to walk around to the backside of this property and investigate it for themselves.

For a few moments, the outside security light came on as the team walked past the sensor and then switched back off, which is what a motion-activated security light is supposed to do. After a couple of minutes, though, Steve noticed a small red laser light that was following their every move. Wherever they walked, it would follow. He quickly pointed it out to the rest of the team, who were all at a loss to understand where it was coming from. As Steve was a military man and familiar with most weapons, his first impression was that someone was pointing a gun at them, but as the movement of the laser was extremely erratic, they were not so sure of this being the case.

They asked Ellen and Tim if there was anyone who lived in the neighborhood that might own a gun and would point it at them in such a threatening manner, perhaps in an attempt to scare them off the property. "Definitely not," Ellen said, "because we have talked to every resident in the area—and they too have been experiencing the same thing as us!" The whole experience was very strange, and the team was unable to draw any conclusions for this type of paranormal activity.

A few days after the investigation, Matthew researched the history of the surrounding area on which the properties had been built to see if there was anything that could possibly be linked to the hauntings. Interestingly enough, he managed to locate a police report that stated that the authorities had unearthed a man's dead body less than two miles from Ellen and Tim's home. Although there was no definite way to prove this, the team's thought was that the man's dead body might be a possible connection to the haunting, if only a slight one.

Conclusion

This case was an unusual one to say the least, as it's not too often that you hear of a haunting both *in and outside* of the home. The paranormal activity here was extremely diverse, and on the surface, seemed unrelated to each other, apart from the diminishing water levels in the fish tank and the sudden appearance of water puddles in a totally different part of the house.

As for the candles on the stairs, the question remains if there was a connection to the couple's religious beliefs, or if indeed, it was an act of ghostly attention seeking on behalf of the spirit. Nevertheless, it did raise a few eyebrows and some thought-

provoking questions, as did the erratic movement of the pendulum swinging back and forth over the child's poster.

The red laser light that the team witnessed at the next-door property was very interesting also. It seemed to be totally out of place, and although many of the neighbors had witnessed this phenomenon for themselves, it still raises the question as to where the light source originated. No one had the answer that night, as the strange laser light was only ever seen operating by itself in the vicinity and appeared to display an intelligence all of its own. LVSSI did perform their usual house cleansing at the request of Ellen and Tim, and were able to successfully remove the spirit from the house...at least from the inside.

7

The Mystery Gunshot!

Location: *Boulder City, Las Vegas, Nevada*
Paranormal Activity: *Voices, Residents Being Awakened by Spirits, Moving of Objects, and Unusual Light Activity*
Investigators: *Matthew Winn, Tina and Steve Carlson, Nancy Riggs, and LVSSI Trainees*

If you ever ask for a sign from a spirit, you had better be prepared for the unexpected. As LVSSI experienced during this ghost investigation, be careful what you ask for because you just might receive it in a way that you had never anticipated!

Cynthia was a middle aged woman who lived with her six-year-old son and her mother in a Boulder City apartment, situated in an old part of the Las Vegas town. Her apartment was also acting as a residence for what appeared to be two ghosts, and although the apartment was large enough for three people, five was definitely pushing it!

Cynthia worked for a very popular Las Vegas magazine and noticed that LVSSI was being featured in a current edition. After reading their interview of how these folks are *real life ghost-busters* here in Las Vegas, she decided to contact them about her own personal supernatural experiences.

"I have some very strange supernatural things going on in my apartment and I don't know what to do about it," Cynthia explained, adding, "I just read your interview in the magazine, and as I also work for the publication, I thought that I should call you to see if you could investigate my home."

LVSSI were happy to assist Cynthia, and after a preliminary meeting had taken place, they made arrangements for a full investigation of her home.

Once the team arrived, Cynthia began telling them all the details of what she, her son, and her mother had been experiencing. One of the ghosts had been calling out her son's name in the middle of the night, along with various disturbances of bumping and knocking that would awake everyone else in the process. As most of this activity was happening in the bedrooms, this was one of the first places the team spent a considerable amount of time investigating.

They started with the boy's bedroom as he had been hearing his name called out over and over, and they decided to use the dowsing rods and ask a series of general questions to see if there were any wandering spirits hanging around in there. The results proved unsuccessful. Not a soul answered. The room just appeared normal and undisturbed by any ghostly behavior, but on entering Cynthia's bedroom, things were very different. There was an immediate sense of strange happenings in there. Furthermore, the team felt the room to be very unhappy. It felt that the spirit was not happy with the situation that it was in...that it appeared to be stuck here. Tina, being what she terms as an empathic rather than a psychic, felt that this spirit was indeed a relative. And in the master bedroom, where Cynthia's mother slept, Tina also felt the presence of the spirit to be a relative.

The team entered the master bedroom, and Tina sat on the floor trying to collect her thoughts and feelings of who this spirit might be. She had a strong sense that this was definitely a woman, and went on to describe her and what she was seeing in her mind's eye. As Tina continued with the description of the spirit, Cynthia's mother became very upset and started to cry.

"Oh, that's my mother you're describing," she said.

"Well, she has a message for you," Tina replied. "She is saying that you need to let go of the guilt. What do you think she means by that?" Tina asked.

Cynthia's mother began to explain how during her own mother's life she felt that she had never done enough for her and that she was still feeling the pain, guilt, and the heartache from this. Suddenly, she became very reluctant to talk about it any further, as she was just so upset about the situation.

"Well, she wants to tell you again to please let go of the guilt, and that she will always love you no matter what because you are her daughter," Tina said.

One thought of why this lovely Grandmother spirit of Cynthia's may have initially come through to contact her mother was because Cynthia's mother had kept the bedroom furniture that once belonged to her mother and it may have been a case that this spirit family member was very much attached to it. Some time ago, before this lady had crossed over into the spirit world, she would awake the household every morning to be sure that they all got off to work on time. But after she passed away, the family's work schedule changed and yet she still continued to wake them up at exactly the same time every morning.

All of the family was feeling so physically tired and exhausted from being woken up so early, and this activity had to stop! Tina spoke to the Grandmother's spirit and asked that she be respectful of the family and allow them to all sleep at the times they were meant to be sleeping. She also let her know that all of the family acknowledged her presence in the home, but to let them live peacefully. At this moment, the team was able to persuade her to leave the home.

However, in Cynthia's bedroom, things were very different. Nancy and the team wandered into her room to find out the reason why they felt that the spirit in here was so unhappy. Nancy took out the dowsing rods to ask a series of simple questions and began by asking if the spirit was happy.

"No!" was the immediate reply through the rods.

They all had a strong sense that this spirit was indeed a male relative, and as these questions were being directed to him, the team decided to ask the entity for a sign of who he was. As a direct result of what happened, this question later became an absolute protocol of what NOT to ask during future investigations.

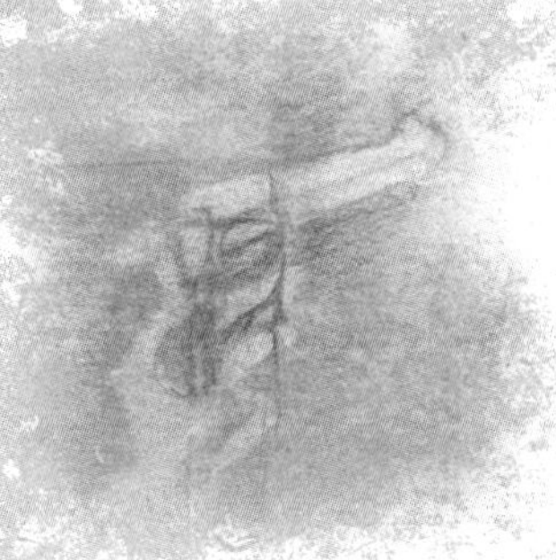

Just as they were asking him to give them a sign, there was a sudden *BANG*... and a loud and deafening gunshot reverberated throughout the entire apartment! It was so intensely piercing to everyone's ears and terrified them all to death! An investigator who had been standing on the family's porch suddenly ran inside the apartment, shouting, "What the hell was that?" After everyone shouted out that they didn't know, he quickly ran back outside to see if anyone may have been driving by the neighborhood, possibly a drive-by shooting? It might have been the result of some natural cause, but nothing presented itself.

A trainee also ran into the room where the team was standing, asking, "Was that a gunshot I just heard?" They were all so terribly shook up over this for quite some time afterwards, and their ears were hurting and ringing! The team reasoned that if the gunshot had happened outside in the neighborhood, it would only have taken moments for the police to arrive; after all it was Las Vegas! So the team all agreed on the fact that the sound was definitely more confined to the inside of the apartment—and that everything had been peaceful up until they asked the spirit to give them a sign.

Everyone in the room felt that there was a huge amount of energy associated with this mysterious gunshot—the atmosphere was highly charged—and they sensed that spirit thought it to be funny to play this kind of a joke on them. When Tina asked Cynthia if she had any idea of who this male relative might be, she commented that her uncle had recently died and he was, in fact, an avid gun collector. It was most likely him who was visiting their home.

It was only later after the investigation that the team was able to laugh about the mysterious gunshot scenario, which, at the time, scared them all half to death and took them all by surprise. Through performing their routine house cleansing, which was directed in particular at Cynthia's uncle, they were able to successfully remove his spirit from her apartment. In regards to Cynthia's Grandmother, they decided not to be as intense with the cleansing in removing her lovely spirit, as the family was not scared or bothered by her presence in any way. To the contrary, they actually felt comfort in having her around. But the team was direct in addressing any other wandering spirits that may have also been residing in the apartment that the team had not come into contact with.

In hearing from the family some weeks later, Cynthia mentioned to the team that her Grandmother would still pay them regular visits during certain hours of the day, and that she would frequently call out their names and move various objects just to remind them that she was still very much present in their home. Of course, they would give her the validation that she needed from them, but there were definitely no more gunshots for the family to report!

Conclusion

When one spirit is present in the home, it's very easy for another to quickly follow. It's difficult to conclude which spirit found its way into Cynthia's home first as they were both related to her. The gunshot was the most bizarre thing that LVSSI ever had happen to them in all their investigations. Because this had happened, they decided they should never ask for a sign from a spirit again.

Spirits will go to any lengths to let you know that they're present, and asking for a sign can be quite a dangerous thing to do as you never know how they're going to present it, but once they do, you have to deal with it in the most sensible and logical of ways.

As this was an investigation during the early months of LVSSI's newly formed paranormal career, this meant that their equipment was pretty much limited. The use of the dowsing rods was the main piece of equipment used in this particular investigation, which allowed them the opportunity of communicating with the spirits.

KESARA

8

Lost Girl

Location: *Nellis Air Force Base, Nevada*
Paranormal Activity: *Pulling of Blankets Off the Bed, Moving Children's Toys, and Moving Various Items*
Investigator: *Tina Carlson*

Very often when people purchase antiques, they are not aware of the possibility that a lingering spirit may still be attached to them. So, upon bringing the item or items home, the spirit then unleashes itself...only to cause all kinds of paranormal havoc as this next ghost investigation demonstrates.

When Tina lived at the Nellis Air Force Base back in 2004, she had a close friend who lived just across the street from her named Kathy. Kathy's husband, like Tina's, was a military man who was away from home in Iraq at the time paranormal activity began manifesting in their home. Like a lot of people, Kathy was an avid antique collector and would spend much of her spare time in and out of local antique stores searching for the most interesting and eye-catching of antiques that she could possibly find, whether it happened to be furniture, photographs, or whatever it would be that called out to her.

One day she approached Tina and said to her anxiously, "You've got to come over to my house Tina...because I've got some really weird activity going on."

Although Kathy was a good friend of Tina's, Tina knew that she had a passion for the paranormal side of life, but was also aware that Kathy had an overactive imagination that would sometimes get the better of her, so, at this point, she wasn't to sure of the validity of what Kathy said she was experiencing in her home. "Well, if you do have a ghost in your house, just talk to it. Find out why it's there and see if it answers you," Tina suggested. She even gave Kathy some ideas of what to say to this supposed resident ghost!

But Kathy's communication with the ghost didn't seem to help matters any, so one night she paid Tina another visit and this time really stressed the importance of her situation. "Tina, you *really* have to come over to my house because *something* is definitely going on. I'm seeing things out of the corner of my eye, it's short and tiny, and I don't have a clue what it is and it's freaking me out." This time Tina felt that perhaps there really was a problem and went over to the house to check things out for herself.

Kathy began telling her of how the family pets were also reacting to this strangeness. She had a couple of basset hounds that would howl frequently when they sensed the spirit around them and they didn't like to be in certain parts of the house, especially in the room where Kathy kept her antiques.

Also, her young son, who was only four-years-old at the time, would say, "Mom, there's someone here. There's somebody in our house." He would constantly experience having his bed covers pulled off him during the night, and although he wasn't scared by it, being so young he just didn't understand what was happening.

Kathy's rocking chair would often move backwards and forwards all by itself, and she was constantly finding doors open all through the house.

Tina decided to sit in the dining room in Kathy's recliner to gather her thoughts and feelings together of who this spirit might be that was causing the disturbances. Within moments, and quite unexpectedly, the chair that Tina was sitting in was suddenly pulled back with such a force, it almost tipped over! It took her totally by surprise and she felt that there was some unseen presence sharing her space. After taking a few moments to compose herself, she happened to glance over to the dining room table, which was an eight-piece set. Suddenly, all of the eight chairs at the exact same time tipped in towards the table! The backs of the chairs were literally resting against the table.

Kathy also managed to see this happen and quickly said, "See, I told you...I told you something was happening in here. Whatever it is, it's done the very same thing a few times."

Shocked and at a loss for words, Tina knew that she had to be as logical as possible about what she had just witnessed and wanted to eliminate as many possibilities as she could. She quickly asked Kathy where the dogs and the children were in the house. Kathy said that the dogs were outside and the children were playing in another room, so neither one could have contributed to this strange event happening. It was the most terrifying and yet unbelievable thing to see—and Tina actually *saw* it happen with her very own eyes. The unfortunate thing about it was that Tina had no investigative equipment with her that night because she initially went to Kathy's house only to see what she could sense there. Admittedly, she still hadn't been sure that what Kathy was actually seeing was real phenomena.

Tina asked to be left alone in the room for a few moments so that she could try to connect with the spirit and get a feel for its energy. She wanted to know why it was present and what might have caused it to push the chair she was sitting on and tip the other chairs forward. She began to see in her mind's eye a little girl between three and four years old...the same age as Kathy's son. She had blonde hair with a huge decorative bow in it and was crying, which in turn made Tina cry as this little girl's emotions began to wash over her. Tina started to talk to her mentally, asking the little girl why she was there.

"I can't find my family,"
the little girl said.

"I don't know where they are...

and I'm here because
I think they're here.

I can see them here."

Tina started to think to herself that this particular housing base wasn't really that old, and that this little lost girl had to be from way back, many centuries ago, possibly the Victorian era by the look of her clothes.

Tina continued to talk with her and tried to console her by saying that her family was waiting on the *other side* and that she should go to them...as they wanted to guide her on her way to the place where she was supposed to be.

But the little girl told Tina that she was too scared to go anywhere else because she didn't know what was beyond that point, and she didn't want to wander off on her own—most especially because she said that she could see her family there in the house.

Tina was becoming somewhat confused at this and thought to herself: How could this little girl see her family in this house? Tina did not sense any other spirits in the home whatsoever—only the little girl. She asked Kathy if she knew what any of this meant.

"Well, you know, funnily enough all of this activity started when I brought these antique photographs home," Kathy said, handing them all to Tina.

As Tina flicked through a number of photographs, standing right there in one of them was the exact little girl surrounded by her family. It was evident to Tina that this is what the little girl was referring to about seeing her family in the house—and that she didn't want to leave the known surroundings for the unknown. Her family must have crossed over a very long time ago, but it was apparent that since the photograph was in the house the little girl assumed her family was to! She was stuck between the two worlds, wandering around in search for her beloved family.

Tina knew exactly what she had to do. She found an ashtray and emptied cooking sage in it, lit it, and walked through Kathy's house telling the little girl that her mommy and daddy were waiting for her on the other side...ready for her to *cross over* where they would be waiting with open arms...and that she wouldn't be lost anymore. The short cleansing was evidently a success because, before Tina left the house that night, everything was calm, peaceful, and back to normal—as it had been before Kathy ever brought the antique photographs into her home. Tina was satisfied with the result of the cleansing, and happy to know that she was able to assist this little anxious child to be where she needed to be, safely back with her loving family in the spirit world.

Conclusion

The best advice one can give when purchasing any antique items is to thoroughly have them cleansed *before* bringing them into your home. As this investigation showed, it's not only adult spirits that can attach themselves to antiques, but child spirits can also find a way of doing the same. Never under-estimate the power of what any ghost or spirit can do, and as you read in this chapter, the whole event of the chair tipping was an incredibly powerful feat—even for a young spirit child. They will stop at nothing to prove their presence in your home.

9

House of Spirits

Location: *Summerlin, Las Vegas, Nevada*
Paranormal Activity: *Numerous Spirits, Banging Sounds, Knocking on Windows, Footsteps, and Voices*
Investigators: *Tina Carlson, Nancy Riggs, and Matthew Winn*

Most people are of the impression that it's only old houses that collect unwanted spirits, but this is not the case. The family in this next ghost investigation had brought a brand new property—and found that there was an abundance of active spirits that would congregate in their new home.

There are many beautiful and scenic areas to live in Las Vegas, and Summerlin is definitely one of them. Surrounded by magnificent mountains—the Red Rock Canyon in particular—this area boasts a prime location for any Las Vegas resident. It was in 2004 that the Dean family had their custom home built here, an older family of three. Alice Dean was in her late sixties and her son, Paul, and daughter, Claudia, in their mid forties.

Their beautiful new home was somewhat still under construction when they moved in, but they were eager to enjoy their new life in such a charming location. But within a very short space of time of settling into their home, Mrs. Dean's son developed an unexpected health problem and, due to various complications of the heart, suddenly died of a heart attack. Devastated by this sudden circumstance, it took the family quite some time to come to terms with his death. After months of still not fully getting over his passing, the family had little choice but to try and pick up their lives and carry on in their new home without the presence of Alice's son—or so they thought!

It all started one day when the family began hearing strange banging sounds in both the bathrooms and the bedrooms, but could never figure out what was causing it. Some of the family members had actually experienced physical interaction—and had been *slapped* and *pushed* by an unseen force on a number of occasions! As you can imagine, they were very shaken by this aggressive and physical behavior.

Doors in the house would frequently open and close, and televisions would always switch themselves on and off at various times of the day and night. There was much ghostly activity in Alice's bedroom where objects would be moved around constantly. She would also happen to see strange shadows frequenting this room that was her most treasured place of retreat. Even though there were no young children living in the house, Mrs. Dean and Claudia would often hear children's voices in certain parts of their home.

Their four dogs were mainly kept outside, but were always growling and barking at something...whatever it was, it always held itself back from being seen. At one point there was pounding on the windows, which was so severe that the family had to call the police because they were convinced that an intruder was trying to break into their home! Claudia had tried to solve the ghost activity herself with an informal cleansing; scattering salt all around the inside of the house and speaking sacred prayers, but neither seemed to help as the plethora of supernatural activity was still very much present.

Searching on the Internet for someone who could help them free their home of the haunting, Claudia found the website of LVSSI and immediately contacted them. After the initial preliminary meeting had taken place, LVSSI arrived at the Deans' home and Claudia described all that was happening there. Alice remained pretty quiet throughout the entire conversation, but fully understood why the team were there and had total faith in their efforts to rid the paranormal from her home.

Alice had always felt really uncomfortable living among the activity—as anyone would. Whatever was dwelling in her new home, she just wanted it to be gone. The team decided to begin their investigation in Claudia's bedroom, and noticed a collection of books that evidently showed her interest in psychics and the paranormal. This may have been why she already knew how to cleanse the house with the scattering of the salt around the property and repeatedly saying prayers in her own attempt to rid the house of the ghost.

Claudia was eager to point out the television to the team, which was placed at the end of the bed. "That TV has a mind of its own, you know...it just keeps switching on and off, and throughout the night I'll suddenly wake up and see the remote control being thrown across the room!" she said.

As Tina listened intently to what Claudia was saying, she sat on the edge of the bed trying to get a feel for the room. Everyone else gathered around with their own thoughts and questions. Suddenly, without any warning, Tina found herself being pushed off the bed! She landed on the floor with a loud thump, and strangely enough, ended up facing towards the bed!

The rest of the team looked across at her with such a bewildered and shocked look. "What just happened?" they asked.

Just then, out of nowhere, there appeared a strange whitish-grey mist. The team watched this mist manifest momentarily around Tina before starting to take photographs of the phenomena. They managed to capture it on film before it totally vanished. The only conclusion that they could come up with was that this strange phenomenon was possibly something called ectoplasm. This is an immaterial or ethereal substance usually whitish in color that appears to show the presence of a spirit or a ghost.

Tina started to laugh at the immediate situation she found herself, and in fact, the whole team had previously been laughing about a few light-hearted comments that referred to Paul, Alice's son, so they thought that perhaps it was he who was listening in on them and who had pushed Tina off the bed! Tina later discovered some bruising to her ribs, which caused her some pain, even though strangely enough she was pushed from her lower back area.

The second room they investigated belonged to Alice's deceased son. This room was totally untouched, remaining like a shrine after his passing. Mrs. Dean and Claudia made it clear that they did not want the team spending too much time in this room as everything had been left just as it was prior to his death and the team respected their wishes.

Nancy sat on the bed, trying to get a sense of what had been happening in there. Within moments, she started to experience a dull pain in her head and then...a strange feeling in her chest. This was always a sure sign to Nancy that a spirit was trying to communicate with her. She had to be very careful, though, as sometimes she had a tendency to allow a spirit to openly talk through her, which was not an ideal thing to do. The team would frequently remind her to never let a spirit inside her head...for her to always be the one in control.

Still aware of the presence of Mrs. Dean's son in spirit, Nancy began feeling all of the symptoms that he had felt at the time of his death. She started to experience real intense pain to her left eye and then to her whole face and head, followed by pain in her chest area, which made her become extremely short of breath. As the team later discovered from talking with Alice, as her son fell to the floor during his heart attack, he hit his face on the dresser and that was why he was giving Nancy the discomfort to her face and upper body.

At this point, Nancy felt it urgent and important to express his message to the family, but as she began, they became very upset—as they were reminded of not being present the day he passed away. Still, Mrs. Dean's son felt it important to come through and speak to them...to say that he was okay and still very much present in their house.

When Paul was alive, he was very much a quiet man, often staying in his room for the majority of the time that he was in the house. Some of the things that the family had been experiencing made them originally believe it was him causing all of the uneasiness in the home, but they quickly dismissed this because it was not his typical behavior or personality. It didn't make any sense to them, especially since the family often heard young children's voices laughing, which could not possibly have been Alice's son, along with the knocking on the outside windows that they categorically said he would not do.

Over a series of months both Mrs. Dean and Claudia had seen several dark figures in their home. At first they weren't so sure whether it was Alice's son or not. But there were other signs that convinced Alice and Claudia that it could not possibly be him. Plus, there was no reason why he would haunt the entire house as a mischievous spirit. After the team listened to them convey their personal feelings of Alice's son, they moved on to the computer room where they discovered it to be full of various boxes from the family's move. After a while of being in the room, it appeared that no ghostly activity seemed to be showing itself, so they left this room and headed to Alice's bedroom.

Alice loved to get involved with arts and crafts, and in a corner of her room, was a small sewing area where she could relax and enjoy her hobby. There was a mirror hanging on one of the walls, and before long, they all witnessed an entity *in this mirror* walking back and forth across the room. Tina shouted out to them.

"There *HE* is! *He's* there in the mirror!"

They quickly grabbed their cameras to take photographs of this dark shadowy figure, but unfortunately, as is most often the case, photographs taken of certain images reflected in mirrors don't usually turn out too well because the camera's flash washes most of the image away. The team got the distinct impression that this spirit was a completely different one from those that were also haunting the house, and the EMF sensor did pick up the spirit's movements, verifying for the team and the family that this entity was definitely present.

There was yet another spirit that would walk around the outside of the property...as the family would hear its footsteps on many occasions. But whenever they peered out the window or opened the door, no one was ever there. These mystery footsteps were heard while LVSSI was at the house—and they too could actually *hear* them on the graveled path area. As the dogs had also heard the footsteps and were now barking frantically, Tina asked Claudia to check on them and to try and calm them down. But as soon as Claudia went outside, not a soul was to be seen. It was almost like the spirit was playing a game with her because as soon as she came back into the house, the footsteps started all over again. The team quickly looked through the window to see if anyone could be seen, but, once again, no one was there. However, the team was able to capture the recording of these footsteps on tape.

As the investigation was turning out to be quite a lengthy one—due to so much spirit activity—Alice quickly became tired and expressed the need to sleep, so the team cleansed her room first using only sage as she had allergies and the team didn't want her room to be overpowered with odors that might interfere with her getting some rest. Paranormal activity had really started to stir more than usual that night, and the team wondered if them being there was causing the spirits to act mischievous.

The living room was the next place of investigation—a beautiful, spacious room with tall ceilings that was connected to the dining area. As they walked around this huge room, they were drawn to the front door area. Hanging on the wall close by was a mirror and an antique sword. The team got the sudden urge to randomly take photographs here. They also felt there was something not quite right with this area. Their EMF device was strongly fluctuating back and forth, confirming that the energy was indeed very intense. They thought there could possibly be lay-lines in this area, but would investigate that later.

Nancy wandered over to one of the chairs, picked up the television remote control, and sat down for a moment, placing the remote on a table by the side of the chair as she did so. After a few minutes, she got up and started walking over to a different part of the room. As soon as her back was turned, she heard a loud thump. She quickly looked back and was surprised to see that the remote control was now on the floor!

As all the team was now together in the living room gathering their thoughts, Tina sat on the couch and tried to sense what might be going on in this room while letting the energy of the room naturally guide her. Within moments, she became very emotional and started to cry. She became a little embarrassed by this as she never liked to show her emotions in front of the team, but they totally understood. They all told her that she should do whatever her feelings compelled her to do.

"Pick up the dowsing rods, Nancy, and see if there's any spirit activity in here," Tina said...but not much happened other than a faint flicker of the rods. Both Nancy and Tina felt at that point that there was something definitely trying to communicate with them. Matthew suggested that Nancy kneel down lower to the floor resting on her knees to see what would happen, and literally within a minute, Tina connected with the presence of a spirit—the spirit of a young girl.

"Yes, it's a child," Tina said.

The kneeling down close to the floor definitely helped to connect with her energy. Now the rods were moving freely on their own accord, connecting with the unseen energy of the spirit, and the team was now able to question the child without any difficulty.

"She wants her family," said Tina. "She can't find her family."

Tina conveyed to the little girl that her family was not in the house, but she was surprised to feel what appeared to be some kind of a restraining situation with this young spirit. As Tina, Nancy, and Matthew started to intuitively connect with the circumstance at hand, they quickly discovered that there was yet *another entity* present in the room with the child—and that it was definitely holding the child back.

"They won't let her go," Tina said anxiously. "They're not going to let her go."

The situation very much reminded them of the famous scene from the "Poltergeist" movie, when the psychic medium tried to convince the entity that it must let the child go, and they all shouted at the same time.

"Go now... go to the light!"

It took every single ounce of energy from them all to tell this child spirit to go towards the light. Matthew was still directing the child to the "light" while Tina shouted out to the other spirits to let the child go.

Matthew: "Just go to the light."

Tina: "You let her go *NOW!*"

At that moment, Nancy could see in her mind's eye the little girl being embraced by her loved ones in the light. Suddenly the energy in the room totally changed into one of complete calmness. They did it! They managed to free the young child from the grasp of this other entity that was holding her back, but not without them all feeling mentally and physically exhausted at the same time. The investigation had taken a full six hours, and they realized their intentions of wanting to strongly cleanse the house and make sure that their clients were put at ease from any further hauntings.

They started their cleansing by the front door where they had felt the strong possibility of lay-lines. A dowsing expert that they had met some time ago had shown them how to work with and successfully

close lay-lines. As soon as they did this, they all *felt* the energy portal immediately close and their EMF device, which had now stopped flashing, proved that they had completed the task. They cleansed the family's house more intensely than others in previous investigations due to the myriad of ghost activity that dwelled there. They covered the entire house—top to bottom—with salt, scattering it around all the doors and windowsills to seal out all the negative energy, and repeated their sacred prayers to confirm their actions.

A week or so later, they contacted the Dean family to check if their home was now ghost free. Alice told the team that she realized that her son was still very much present around the house. Every so often she and Claudia would experience certain feelings and witness various clues that he was still there. All the other paranormal activity—the mysterious footsteps, noises, dark shadowy figures, and the children's laughter—had now ceased completely, and both Mrs. Dean and Claudia were now relieved that their home was released from the paranormal.

Conclusion

This was an extreme case of intense haunting to say the least! The team concluded that there were perhaps as many as eight or ten spirits gathered here all at one time, but they weren't sure if they were there to help the spirit child or assist the other spirit that was restraining her.

Paranormal interaction with any family can take its toll and become extremely frustrating and difficult. In this case, Claudia and her mother felt the strain on their own relationship very much. Fortunately, they were able to patch things up towards the end of the investigation and continued to have a warm and loving mother-daughter relationship once again.

Photographs that the team had taken throughout the six-hour investigation showed a number of unexplainable images on them. A couple of them in particular revealed some form of light source streaking across the room while another showed the presence of a strange whitish-grey green substance, which LVSSI referred to as possible ectoplasm. Other photos that were taken showed what appeared to be a number of orbs, but the team later concluded that the orbs looked to be more like that of air-bourne dust particles rather than genuine orb phenomena.

Oddly enough the team didn't capture any EVPs from this particular investigation, even though Mrs. Dean and Claudia had repeatedly heard the voices of young children. The team did record the footsteps and knocking sounds that the family had so frequently heard. The EMF meters also showed a high amount of energy fluctuations that indicated spirit or spirits to be present.

10

Man from the Past

Location: *Swenson, Las Vegas, Nevada*
Paranormal Activity: *Terrorization of Spirit, Moving of Objects, Noises, Calling out Names, Problems with Electrical Appliances, and Footsteps*
Investigators: *Tina Carlson, Nancy Riggs, and Matthew Winn*

Ghosts don't seem to have any limitations, and while some spirits are anxious to make contact either through positive or negative intentions, in this ghost investigation a male spirit from the 1950s era made contact in a very deliberate attempt to terrorize and plague a seventeen-year-old girl in an extremely terrifying way.

Teresa and Julia are two sisters ages twenty-four and seventeen, who share an apartment in the East Central area of Las Vegas. Their residential community was built in the late 1960s-early 1970s. What was interesting about their building was that it was designed to be like that of a hotel with the apartments facing each other along a corridor that ran between them.

In 2007 the building was purchased by a new development company that re-modeled the property, but unfortunately it didn't really enhance its appearance that much, and the building still remained looking somewhat run down. However, though only having lived in the apartment for a year and a half, it was very evident to the sisters that supernatural activity was indeed present and abundant—for an entire eighteen months they lived in total fear of the ghostly interaction that occurred on a weekly basis.

Originally they had contacted another paranormal investigations group to help them with their ghost situation, but as very little was done to remove these unwanted spirits, they quickly became unimpressed by their investigation style and lack of professionalism. Both sisters were left feeling somewhat let down and that no one could help them—not even a paranormal investigation group! They believed that they had no choice but to continue living with this ghostly phenomena.

But after living with these supernatural occurrences for some eighteen months or more, they decided enough was enough! They were so fed up with the hauntings, which left them feeling so terrified, tormented, and upset...that they could no longer tolerate the activity. It was all too much to handle—the whispering voices, hearing a spirit hum and footsteps, the calling out of their names, seeing shadows, and the constant moving of objects on their computer desk. But what bothered them more than anything else was the *physical interaction* from the spirit. Whenever Julia, the younger sister, was in the bathroom taking a shower, a hand would manifest from out of nowhere and try to grab her *through* the shower curtain! The plastic curtain would physically move from the spirit's hand pressing against it, trying to reach for her. She was absolutely terrified and had no idea of what was doing this.

There were also many instances where the spirit would tamper with the water temperature, always back and forth from hot and cold. Then one day, to their horror, they *saw* the *full shadow of a person* leaning against the frame of the bathroom door...just standing there watching them. Sometimes, when they were getting dressed or undressed, the spirit would be hanging around watching, but they were also aware that this spirit seemed to target Julia more than her sister.

One of the sisters happened to be fascinated with the music icon Elvis Presley and had a number of pictures of him hanging on the wall. One morning when they awoke, they found one of the large framed pictures of Elvis broken and sitting upright against the wall—totally opposite from the wall it had fallen from. There was a small table close to the picture that had a number of glass ornaments on it—little trinkets and glass dolphins—but nothing on the table was ever touched or damaged, and at the time, they never heard the picture falling off the wall.

One day, this spirit decided to reveal its presence a little more by *appearing in the bathroom mirror* and what they saw confirmed their suspicions—this was indeed a male spirit wearing a baseball cap, but with the bill of the cap covering his entire face. He made

every effort to make his presence known as often as he possibly could...especially just to terrorize and torment Julia.

But there was a second spirit in their apartment; a *Grandmother figure* that they would catch a glimpse of from time to time. They felt that she had occupied their apartment before the male spirit was ever present because, though they had witnessed objects being moved around and heard whispering and their names being called out, their apartment had actually been very calm and peaceful—nothing malevolent ever happened. But once the male spirit made his presence known, the energy in their apartment totally changed.

It's very true to say that spirits do often attract other spirits, and once one finds its way into your space, it's very much an open door for another to quickly follow. The sisters had periodically caught glimpses of the female's clothing, which appeared to be from the early 1900s, but she, unlike the male entity ,was quite elderly and much more of a happy go-lucky spirit.

Teresa, through her Internet research, had managed to locate the website of LVSSI, and although the sisters were initially reluctant and unsure whether to pursue finding another investigation team to help them, they also knew that their lives would continue in total misery and fear unless they got help once and for all. After a preliminary meeting, they arranged for the team to visit their apartment and start of the investigation. The girls explained to them how they were actually believers in ghosts, but neither one of them had prior experience of dealing with a haunting. Teresa recalled how she thought that her mother may have had some paranormal experiences herself, but could never really speak to her about it in any detail, as her mother's day job always kept her busy on the road as she was a truck driver.

As the team prepared for their investigation, they began by setting up their equipment. Teresa placed their pet dog, cat, and bird in another room so that the team could walk freely through the apartment. Both pets had experienced a few strange things and would often just stare at nothing...or what seemed to be nothing. Animals are so sensitive when it comes to the paranormal world—more so than humans—and there are many cases of how pet owners have described their animals simply staring at *something* and their *eyes following* the unseen whenever it happened to move. There's no doubt that pets always give us a sign that we're not alone.

The team set up a piece of equipment in Julia's bathroom, which was where the activity was mainly occurring. It was a new device they had purchased called a remote view camera. This would allow them to see any shadows of spirit—on a small hand-held monitor—that might be looming around in a particular room while the team was physically in another. In this case, they were standing in one of the bedrooms.

After a short time, the team noticed that Tina was becoming increasingly agitated, as she started to rock back and forth while sitting on the bed. Matthew was a little concerned about this and asked if she was feeling okay. Although Tina replied that she was fine, she was actually getting pains in both sides of her head—it was so painful that she started to clench her teeth.

They all knew from her agitation that there was definitely someone present...so they grabbed the dowsing rods to see if they could communicate with the unseen entity. They were sure it was the male spirit that had so frequently been hanging around Julia, but when they held the rods and began to ask questions, he was ever so reluctant to answer.

This spirit was such a strong-minded soul, and felt that the more the team knew about him and his past, the quicker they would want to banish him from the girls' home. Everyone in the team had to be conscious at all times of not becoming a conduit—an open channel allowing him to speak through one of them. They had to keep reminding themselves to remain in the "third person" at all times because, if they became too relaxed, at any moment *he* could find a way to take over their thoughts.

Becoming out of breath, Tina now felt that she was experiencing feelings from a situation when *he* was alive. She sensed that he was running away from something, but what? Nancy thought that maybe he was running away from the law or some other authority figure because in her mind's eye she could also see him being chased. Tina knew this had to be the case, but after a while said that she couldn't go on any further because of all the emotions she was physically feeling.

As Matthew sat seated in one of the chairs, at first he couldn't sense anything, but within moments he suddenly felt an intense agitation start to take over him and the room. All three investigators were now physically feeling like they had been running a long distance in such a short amount of time—and were totally exhausted. This unseen entity was transferring his impressions on them, which a spirit can do often and very easily.

Matthew began asking questions to the spirit, and noticed that as he did, the chair would shake and move all by itself. No matter how many times he asked a question, the spirit would not answer, but since the chair would move, it was a sure sign that *he* was definitely present and *provoking* the situation. Matthew asked Nancy if she wanted to sit in the chair, but she knew that since the rest of the team were experiencing the phenomena, she was the next in line. Nevertheless, she decided to do it and sat there...waiting to see what the spirit would do next.

"Okay, I'm starting to feel the agitation and my heart's beginning to race," she said.

The very next thing Nancy knew was that she was being prodded in her arm by some unseen force—and the chair started to shake yet again. All of them perceived through a mental image that this male spirit was from the 1950s era because of his hairstyle, which was shaped like a "D.A." and was quite greasy and slicked back. Tina, Nancy, and Matthew couldn't help but to feel that he had been beaten up by some mob when he was alive...as they were experiencing severe physical pains to their bodies. Whoever was chasing him were really angry and extremely upset with him. They decided that they would try once again to make contact through the dowsing rods and began with a few simple questions.

Nancy: "Can we take your picture?"
Male Spirit: *"No."*

Tina: "Do you want to leave us a message?"
Male Spirit: *"No."*

Matthew: "Would you tell us your name?"
Male Spirit: *"No."*

Tina: "Will you leave this family alone?"
Male Spirit: *"No."*

At this point the rods were moving with more intensity during the question and answer session. The team sensed him to be very arrogant, in addition to having a real bad attitude. He was a real tough guy who felt that he didn't have to answer any of the questions they were asking him. The team got the impression that he was saying to them:

"Why should I answer your questions?"

"Who are you to ask me these questions?"

"I'm here and you're not going to make me leave."

They knew he was trying to intimidate them and every question asked to him seemed to make him even more arrogant. Once again they got the distinct impression that he was saying to them, "Who are you people? You mean nothing to me." The more the team tried to break him down, the stronger he lashed back at them.

They tried once again to get him to tell them his name, but he was adamant that he was not going to reveal it. But the strange thing was that all of the team had the mental image of the letter "A," followed by a few more letters. Unfortunately they could not determine a name from them.

Meanwhile, the remote view camera sitting by the chair was going absolutely crazy, switching to various channels all by itself. The EMF meter was also now very active, switching continuously to a yellow mode—that confirmed there was some source of unknown energy present. Even though a number of their equipment was showing signs of a real presence, the team knew they were not going to be successful in getting any answers from him, so they decided to pull away from him and focus on the Grandmother figure.

The team felt her spirit to be a good one, very meek and mild, and they sensed that she had a great deal of love for the sisters. Teresa and Julia did not recognize her, but through the team's ability to connect with her, they found out that she was in fact a distant ancestor who had lived *and died* many decades before they were even born. Whenever the team tried to communicate with *her*, asking *her* to validate her presence, they sensed the male entity backing away and retreating to a corner of the room.

It's not usual for multiple spirits to interact with each other, but on this occasion the team had to reinforce the message to this Grandmotherly spirit that *she* was the guardian of the family and, as such, they needed her help with this male entity. They had to persuade her that she had much more power than he did. Once the team managed to convince her of this—and she realized *why* she was present in the home—she seemed to rapidly gain all the power she needed to put this male spirit in his place!

The male spirit was totally shocked that the team had gotten her to acknowledge her strength and power over him...this 1950s bully. He hadn't expected it and knew that the "Grandmother" was out to get him one way or another! The team saw a mental image of him running down the hall and hiding in the bathroom, but the Grandmother spirit quickly followed him—and stayed in there, blocking the door so that he could not make an exit. At this time, the remote view camera was showing signs of extreme spirit activity.

This whole scene that they were envisioning was comical, to say the least. It produced a lot of laughter among the team. They could all see in their mind's eye that this Grandmother figure was going to now take charge—and even slap this male spirit around a little! At this point the team was satisfied that she had taken control of the situation and regained her own power to protect her family.

There was now very little for LVSSI to do, but before they gathered their belongings together, at Julia and Teresa's request, they performed a complete and thorough cleansing of the apartment. But there was one thing remaining before they left that night—they communicated with the Grandmother, *asking her* to stay behind to watch over both Teresa and Julia at all times.

Conclusion

It's not usual for multiple spirits to interact with one another, but this was a case where it seemed necessary for the female spirit to interact with the male spirit...to show her power over his terrorization and torment of Julia. The Grandmother did eventually realize that even though she was in the spirit realm, she still had all of the energy and power that she had when she was alive. She just needed help recognizing it, and once she did, she took charge over the arrogant bully whose presence was definitely not welcome.

LVSSI was never able to find out why the so-called 'mob' had been chasing him when he was alive, but they concluded that this male spirit must have committed some terrible act. They were not sure if it was perhaps something to do with a molestation case or even pedophilia, but they knew for sure that he had experienced a severe beating.

After about a week, LVSSI contacted Teresa and Julia to see if things had improved in their apartment. The cleansing appeared to have been successful, as the male spirit had totally vanished. They were still experiencing the presence of the Grandmother, which did not scare or bother them, as they knew now she was there as a guardian to protect and watch over them for future years to come.

11

Somebody's There!

Location: *Sunrise Mountain, Las Vegas, Nevada*
Paranormal Activity: *A Shadow Person, Footsteps, Whispering, and Knocking Sounds*
Investigators: *Nancy Riggs and LVSSI Trainees*

Considering all the possible methods used in contacting spirits, the Ouija Board® is definitely not a good choice. It's an open invitation for spirits to come into your home and, once there, might choose not to leave. This investigation tells of a family using such a device—and then calling on LVSSI for their help!

In May 2006, Tina Carlson, director of LVSSI, received an email from Glenda Matthews, who lived on a trailer park with her husband and son in the area of Sunrise Mountain. Glenda said that her family was aware of paranormal activity in their home and could LVSSI help to get rid of it. The team set up a preliminary meeting with Glenda to talk about what was going on in her family's home, but on the actual night of the scheduled investigation, personal circumstances arose for Tina, Steve, and Matthew, so they were not able to accompany Nancy on this investigation. But Nancy decided that she would handle this particular case by herself, taking along a few trainees.

The Matthews' home was a mobile one that has been their main place of residence for the past ten years. Behind it, a few hundred yards away, stood a small house that they also owned. Although Glenda did not go into specifics about this house, Nancy had gotten the distinct impression that they had planned on refurbishing it for another family member, but since they never actually completed the project they ended up using it as their laundry and storage facility instead.

Glenda described to Nancy and the trainees about the ghostly activity in her home and said that she had lived with the feeling for quite some time that *somebody* was there. Frequent footsteps and distinct knocking sounds would be heard, light bulbs would rapidly blow out and there were always constant electrical and plumbing issues. In addition, Glenda heard whispering voices, which she took to be evidence that someone wanted to talk with her.

Glenda also told the team about a shadow person that she frequently saw—a man dressed in black that would lean against the wall of the small house—and then he would quickly turn and *walk through it*! Sometimes he would be seen going into and coming out of the master bedroom closet in the mobile home. She had even witnessed him peeking out from behind the mirror on her dresser!

This activity was not confined to just their mobile home though, as they had also witnessed it at the small house. After discussing everything that had happened—and was *still* happening—Glenda asked Nancy where she wanted to start the investigation.

"Let's start with the small house," Nancy replied.

She and the team made their way across to the house while Glenda and her family stayed in the mobile home. Once they took their first step inside, though, they were overwhelmed by the stifling heat, which hit them immediately. Nancy felt that it must have been over one hundred degrees, as there was no air conditioning running in the home. It was obvious that the family was being quite conservative with the use of it, especially since no one lived in there.

At that moment, however, everyone could smell a strange odor that seemed to be different from what the other was smelling. They had no idea where it was coming from. Nancy described it as an old musty smell, while one trainee smelled tobacco, and another described a sweaty smell that reminded her of an odor belonging to an old man. As the team started to wander around, Nancy stood by the clothes dryer and suddenly became disorientated. She felt as if she was about to fall over as her feet became very unsteady and she felt extremely dizzy. She also had the overwhelming feeling that someone was there. She felt an intense pressure in her head and that the ground was moving beneath her.

As this was one of Nancy's earlier investigations, she had no idea that this was how she would feel when spirits were trying to communicate with her. It was only with the passing of time and working on other investigations that she learned to recognize the "symptoms" of a spirit wanting to talk with her, but on this evening, the spirit did not get the opportunity to connect with her as she was not able to mentally open her mind to the possibility of contact.

The team thought that they should split up and explore different rooms of the house and to have what they called their "quiet time alone" during which they tried to find out if there were any spirits present that wanted to communicate with them. But they were out of luck that night as not much spirit activity was brewing.

However, when one of the trainees was standing in the living room area, she noticed an open window that was allowing a cool breeze to blow through the room, yet the breeze was not affecting the curtains—they did not move. Was some unseen force manipulating the surroundings in an effort at showing what it could do? The trainee thought this to be very odd indeed and *sensed* that some unseen entity was definitely present, but it never revealed itself to her.

Nancy, on the other hand, experienced seeing orb phenomena in motion—right in front of the clothes dryer where she had been standing. Could this have been the reason she felt dizzy and disoriented? That spirit wanted to *contact* her and no one else. Nancy decided it was the perfect time to try an experiment called a 'control' in which she placed a small bell and a coin on a white piece of paper. She then traced around the objects and left them sitting on the paper to see if a spirit would try to move them. She placed the control in a secret location so that no one else knew about it and told the spirit, or spirits, to feel free to move the objects if it so desired. When she went to check the results sometime later, the bell had been moved from the circle that was traced around it. Nancy smiled because she knew it was evidence that a spirit was indeed present with them—and *it* knew what she was asking it to do and complied.

Suddenly, the team heard footsteps coming from outside the house. They distinctly heard a light crunching sound on the gravel path around the property. They all ran to the window to see who was out there, but no one was. A thought crossed their minds that maybe it could have been a family member sneaking around to check up on them, but Glenda had assured them that they were going to stay inside the mobile home while the group carried out their investigation in the small house.

As not much activity was occurring in the house, the team felt it time to go back to the mobile home and continue their investigation there. But, before they did, they stepped outside to get some fresh air and to randomly take photographs in the hope that they might capture the presence of a spirit, but Nancy was experiencing sudden problems with her 35mm camera. For some reason, it just didn't want to take any pictures. It would work for a few moments and then it wouldn't, despite having previously changed the batteries. She was convinced that this was spirit intervening and playing around with her.

Once back at the mobile home, Nancy did ask Glenda if either she or anyone in the family had in fact been walking over by the house at any point, as the team had heard definite footsteps outside the property. Glenda, her husband, and son all quickly assured them that they were in the mobile home the whole time.

As the group began exploring the mobile home, it wasn't too long before Nancy discovered an Ouija Board in one of the closets. She wasn't too thrilled to see this kind of communication device, and as the rest of LVSSI was not present that night, she could not consult anyone about it or ask for their advice. She knew that the board was a bad omen and not a good idea for the family to have in their home. She thought to herself that she had only two possible options: she either had to continue with the investigation, or simply leave. She opted to stay and complete the investigation, realizing that it wouldn't be right for her and the others to leave the family in such an unresolved situation.

In search of a resolution to this, Nancy gathered the trainees together and brought their attention to the Ouija Board. One of them told Nancy not to worry as she had learned how to close Ouija Boards and had done it many times before. She explained the process: she would mentally create an energy bubble around the board, working with it until the bubble became so big it covered the board entirely. As Nancy had very little options at this point, she agreed to let the trainee do this.

The team stood and watched, anxiously, as the trainee focused on closing the board. Once done, Nancy and the rest of the group commented that the energy surrounding the board had indeed totally changed. The atmosphere in the mobile home, in general, just felt different. Glenda's son also immediately picked up on the difference. He said that it felt much lighter than it had previously, but, nevertheless, Nancy and the trainees suggested that the family get rid of the Ouija board once and for all and not place it back in the closet.

Nancy felt that a few questions needed to be answered about the board and decided to confront Glenda about it. She especially wanted to know why it was there in the first place. Glenda said that she had owned the board for approximately two years and hadn't used it in a very long time. But she added that she and her son would sometimes dabble with it and made a point of mentioning that she was reluctant to throw it away. Nancy asked if she thought if they had ever contacted any spirits through it, and Glenda admitted that she believed they had as she had witnessed the shadow figure going in and out of the closet and peeking out at her from behind the mirror.

Glenda added that she felt that they had contacted this spirit from a past life connection even though she had no way to validate it—and that *he* had attached himself to her. She felt that the spirit wanted to help and be there for her when it was time for Glenda herself to cross over into the spirit world. She explained to Nancy that she had recently been having health issues, especially with a heart condition that she had for some time.

Nancy, however, felt that this male spirit had been in their home prior to them ever using the Ouija Board and that dabbling with this type of communication device had only enhanced the connection of the spirit to Glenda. Nancy asked the group what they now felt their next step should be, and they quickly came to the conclusion that they should investigate the master bedroom using the dowsing rods...to see if they could connect with the male spirit that Glenda was referring to.

Nancy picked up the dowsing rods and began to ask questions to the spirit. Simple questions were asked, such as: Are you male? Are you a relative? Are you here in this house as a watching capacity? Are you the one that the family has seen peering from behind the mirror? Through all of the positive and negative answers the spirit gave them, the team concluded that *it* was a family member from Glenda's side of the family. *He* has been watching and waiting—and stepping in and out of the closet. The series of questions they had asked helped them to validate that it was indeed Glenda who, in a previous life, had taken care of him and now he wanted to return the kindness.

The team thought it necessary at this point to have some quiet time alone to gather their thoughts; one of the trainee investigators sat in the bedroom while another headed towards the kitchen. Nancy made her way to the main bathroom. It was in here that she asked a question out loud in case a spirit might be listening.

"Are you in here with me?" she asked. "If you are, just let me know."

Suddenly there was a creak in the bathtub—and the tap started to drip uncontrollably and very loudly. It had definitely been quiet in this room when Nancy first stepped in, but as soon as she started to ask her questions the noises began. She knew that someone was there and that she was being watched. The room temperature had also suddenly dropped, and she quickly started to feel goose bumps on her arms.

The team approached Glenda and her family to ask if they would like them to perform a cleansing in the two properties, but Glenda declined the offer as she was certain that the spirit shadow person was to be her relative, and in her own time would be waiting for validation as to exactly who it was. Of course, the team respected Glenda's wish and did not carry out a cleansing, but did close their investigation with a sacred prayer.

Conclusion

As I had stated at the beginning of this chapter, Ouija Boards are often a definite source of contact for negative and unwanted spirits. It also opens the door for them to wander in. Many spirits can be

attracted to your home through this kind of device—and then choose not to leave.

Many of these spirits have a tendency to lie when they come through, and can indeed tell you that they are a close relative when in fact it might not be the case. No matter how you choose to look at this source of communication, you are sending out a vibration that is welcoming any wandering negative spirit to be your next visitor and it's not just limited to spirits—it can also be an open invitation to the demonic realm.

Most people do not know how to protect themselves when using this device. They find themselves running into trouble just like in this case and then seeking to find a quick fix to the problem. The best solution is to avoid Ouija Boards at all costs.

During the team's investigation, they did use the EMF meters, but they also did not seem to over-react under the supernatural circumstances. While no EVPs were captured in this particular investigation, they did collect a series of photographic evidence showing orb phenomena. The main source of communication throughout this investigation was through the use of the dowsing rods, which usually shows success for the team most times.

12

Fox Ridge Park

Location: *Henderson, Las Vegas, Nevada*
Paranormal Activity: *Child's Swing In Local Park Swinging By Itself*
Investigators: *Tina Carlson, Nancy Riggs, Matthew Winn, and LVSSI Trainees*

It has long been rumored that Fox Ridge Park is haunted by the spirit of a young boy. Just after midnight a child's swing can be seen moving back and forth, and if you happen to see the child spirit and look him in the eyes, he will change his face into that of a demon and suddenly disappear...or so the story goes!

In 2005 LVSSI learned of the rumors that a child spirit haunts Fox Ridge Park through the Shadowlands Ghost Organization. It sounded like an interesting case, so they decided to investigate the location to see if the little boy's spirit would indeed appear. They were uncertain as to whether the story was genuine or just a rumor, but nevertheless arranged to undertake a ghost hunt one night just after midnight.

On this night, their equipment included dowsing rods, cameras, audio devices, a video recorder, EMF detector, and even motion sensors. Not sure what to expect, they walked into the park and took a moment to glance around and get a feel for the area, especially at the location where the ghostly activity has been reported to happen. This park is situated in a new subdivision of Henderson, Nevada, a new growth area that proudly offers the park to the local neighborhood residents.

In the area of the park where the paranormal activity has frequently been witnessed, there was a set of four children's swings. One of them was reported to move on its own while the other three remained

completely still. As the reports from people were somewhat sketchy, the team had no idea which swing would actually move, so they chose a swing in the middle of the set, and placed their EMF detector and audio recorder underneath it. The swings were so close to one another—only an inch or so apart—that they felt the equipment was sensitive enough to certainly pick up the activity. They then sat close by under a canopied area...waiting for the moment of truth.

One of the trainees decided that he would use the dowsing rods in a separate location of the park, slightly away from the others, just to see if any activity was occurring elsewhere.

They waited with baited breath, but they didn't have to wait for long...as it wasn't too long before one of the swings actually started to move. Gradually, it started to swing slowly back and forth, and then, with the team looking on in shock, gained momentum. But it wasn't the swing with the equipment placed underneath it moving. The witness reports from the Shadowlands website was unclear as to whether the child spirit chose a different swing each time it frequented the park. There was no breeze whatsoever, so the team knew this to be genuine paranormal activity. If there had been a breeze, surely all four swings would have been affected by it.

They stood up and walked over to the swing, noticing that as soon as they approached it, a definite cold spot covered the area. It was almost like walking into a large freezer as the temperature had drastically dropped. Yet when they took just a couple of steps back from the swing, the cold was gone and the temperature was the regular temp for a Las Vegas night. The team stayed with this experiment for a few moments and then took out their cameras to take a few photographs. The trainee holding the dowsing rods had been experiencing movement with them, but other team members remained watching the swing constantly move back and forth.

Suddenly... the team noticed a police car pull up on the opposite side of the park. Surprised by this, they watched the police officer walk across the park towards them. As he did, the swing came to an abrupt stand still. He first approached the trainee holding the dowsing rods and inquisitively asked, "What are you all doing out here?"

The trainee's answer was blunt and direct. "We're looking for ghosts," he said matter-of-factly.

For a moment there was an awkward silence as the police officer didn't seem to know how to respond. At a seeming loss for

words, the officer turned his direction to Tina. "Are you aware that this park closes at 10 p.m.?" he asked.

"Well, there are no signs in the park," Tina replied, asking to kindly be shown them.

The team had looked for any park signs when they first walked in, but didn't see any. At this point Tina and the police officer were going back and forth, and he made a point of stating that the park's rules and regulations were clearly outlined in their city ordinances.

Tina still insisted that there should be signs visible in the park for the general public to see, but the police officer was now starting to become extremely agitated by all of her questioning and his demeanor changed.

"You have to leave the property right *NOW*," he said abruptly.

Reluctantly but quickly, the team acknowledged his request and packed up their belongings. After all, they didn't want to argue with a Henderson Police Officer—or go to jail, for that matter.

Conclusion

Although this ghost hunt was cut short due to the interruption of the police officer, the initial rumor of Fox Ridge Park turned out to be a factual one. It does indeed appear to be haunted by the spirit of someone who likes to swing to their heart's content after midnight. Although LVSSI witnessed the swing moving back and forth for themselves, none of the team members actually saw the physical appearance of a little boy. If the police officer had not been present, who knows what they might have encountered that particular night.

As for their equipment, the EMF meter did show signs of an unknown presence on the swing—as well as the physical movement of it witnessed by the team—and photographs taken of the area did show activity of orb phenomena at the time.

It's important to mention here that for anyone interested in participating in the search of ghosts in various public places, to always check their hours of visitation as well as any notice for trespassing, and to respect and adhere to them at all times.

13

Our Cemetery

Location: *Southwest Las Vegas, Nevada*
Paranormal Activity: *Shadow People, Banging, Spiritual Attack, and Interference of Walkie-Talkies*
Investigators: *Tina and Steve Carlson, Nancy Riggs, and Matthew Winn*

Cemeteries are extremely popular places for ghost hunting and can very often bring positive results, depending upon the history and the day-to-day spirit activity of them. LVSSI has performed many ghost hunts in cemeteries throughout the Las Vegas area and has become quite attached to a number of them. This particular cemetery is no exception; it holds a special place in their hearts and they often refer to it as Our Cemetery.

This cemetery, however, is somewhat different. It's unlike any other that they have investigated and explored. That's because the perimeter appears to, unmistakably, act as a magical barrier, separating two distinct worlds from one another. Oddly enough, if you stand in the street at the perimeter of the cemetery and take a step onto the grounds, all sounds of the living world completely disappears. No longer will you hear the traffic, the birds, the chirping sound of the crickets, or any other nightly desert sound for that matter—only that of a complete eerie silence. Yet, if you take a step back over the perimeter onto the street, all the usual sounds of the living world immediately spring back to life!

LVSSI has experimented with this perimeter on many occasions and the result has been the same every time. Although they have often seen birds hopping along the fence of the cemetery, not one bird has ever been seen to hop over onto the grounds. No fly, cricket, mosquito, or any other insect can be found in there. In this cemetery, it appears that both the deceased world and the outside living world have a definite separation from each other.

Matthew had driven past the cemetery on a few occasions and thought it would be an interesting place to ghost hunt. When he suggested it to the team, they were eager to take on their first investigation of paranormal activity there—and this particular evening proved to be both active and unforgettable!

It was a warm summer's night with a full moon. Before they began their ghost hunt, they spoke a lengthy prayer of protection, a St. Michaels prayer, followed by the application of sacred oil and holy water to their foreheads. This is a most important routine for them—and one they always carry out at the start of any investigation—as they don't want to be vulnerable to any negative spirits or energy likely to be present. They then walk the grounds picking up any trash along the way or decayed flowers that may have blown across the graves, as they have done in many of their cemetery investigations.

Immediately the team notices the presence of shadow people standing by the perimeter of the fence. There were a dozen or more of them that night just standing and watching them, but once the team acknowledged their presence...*they* would suddenly hide behind the trees and the desert shrubbery. It was as if they were playing a game of hide-and-seek with them, and although their facial features weren't visible, the team heard their distinct footsteps crunching along the gravel. They knew not to approach them because if they did—and crossed over the perimeter—their protection would be gone and they'd be back in the real world.

The team refers to these shadow people as *The Watchers*—full size human adults, dark in color, and indistinguishable from male or female. Through their many years of research, they have learned that they are in fact neither malevolent nor benevolent spirits, but take on a neutral presence. They simply stand guard and observe any human being in the cemetery to make sure that their intentions are nothing but kind. They consider the cemetery to be their sacred property, guarding it and their fellow kindred spirits.

Tina recalls an experience with a shadow person during one of their ghost hunts at a different cemetery, just a short distance from this one. This shadow person stood on the opposite side of the street and proceeded to follow them into the cemetery, walking slightly behind them.

Back at this cemetery and their investigation, Matthew pointed out to both Tina and Nancy that he could hear something that resembled the sound of a body being dragged across the gravel. As soon as he mentioned it, the others too could clearly hear it. They were startled to hear the sound and they wondered, among themselves, who could possibly be out there dragging a body through the desert. It was bizarre to say the least, especially since they knew they were the only human beings there that night!

Now standing at the far side of the cemetery, they distinctly sensed that other spirits were present with them. Tina made a point of telling the spirits that the team knew they were there and asked that they show them proof of their presence. Suddenly, a distinct loud metallic banging sound was heard reverberating throughout the cemetery. It seemed to be coming from a metal flagpole close by that had a chain and a rope attached to it. The team knew that this was their "proof," as they had been there for a whole hour and the entire place had been totally peaceful and quiet up to that point.

Curious to see *if* the sound had come from the flagpole, they tried replicating it by taking hold of the rope and pounding it on the pole. They even threw rocks at it, but nothing seemed to copy the metallic sound that they were hearing. No breeze was present that night, which also ruled out the possibility that the wind was causing the chain and the rope to hit it, and they repeatedly asked the spirit to continue making the sound for them. However, they knew that if they ventured too close to the pole, the sound would stop.

Meanwhile, Steve, Tina's husband, who had been their only source of transportation for their investigations at that time, was sitting in his vehicle just outside the cemetery, studying for an exam in conjunction with his work at the Air Force Base. They were frantically trying to reach him through each of their walkie-talkies to tell him about the shadow people and the mysterious banging sound they had heard, but there was no answer. Steve was parked only a short distance away from them and they tried getting his attention by also waving at him and flashing their flashlights, but it was as if a magical barrier had affected the communication between them—Steve heard and saw nothing.

From the very first time that LVSSI had visited the cemetery, they were pulled towards a certain grave. It appeared to be a double grave due to the size of the mound. On one side of it grew lush green grass; yet on the opposite side, nothing appeared to grow there at all...it was completely dead. The grave itself had an extremely dark and ominous feeling about it, unlike that of any other grave on the property, and a feeling that not all was well with it. The team was of the consensus that whoever or whatever was buried in this grave...was the *personification of ALL evil*. This grave is also marked by a strange looking dead tree, which gives the impression that it's standing guard over it, and even when seeing it from the street, it extends a most unfriendly and eerie invitation to the grave.

At this particular graveside, they always felt sheer terror, fear, and utter gloom. As Tina is a very strong empathic, she especially felt that this buried entity—or whatever it happened to be—was just biding its time, waiting for her or the others to let down their guard, their wall of protection that they had mentally built around them before they even stepped near to it. Tina has always been uncertain as to whether this entity was of a demonic nature, and everytime that she and the team have tried to speak with the entity buried at the lower part of the grave, it has never responded. Tina has actually always been of the impression that perhaps the entity could not speak English.

Another odd thing about the grave was the strange selection of objects placed on it; objects such as twine, a statue of a Chinese

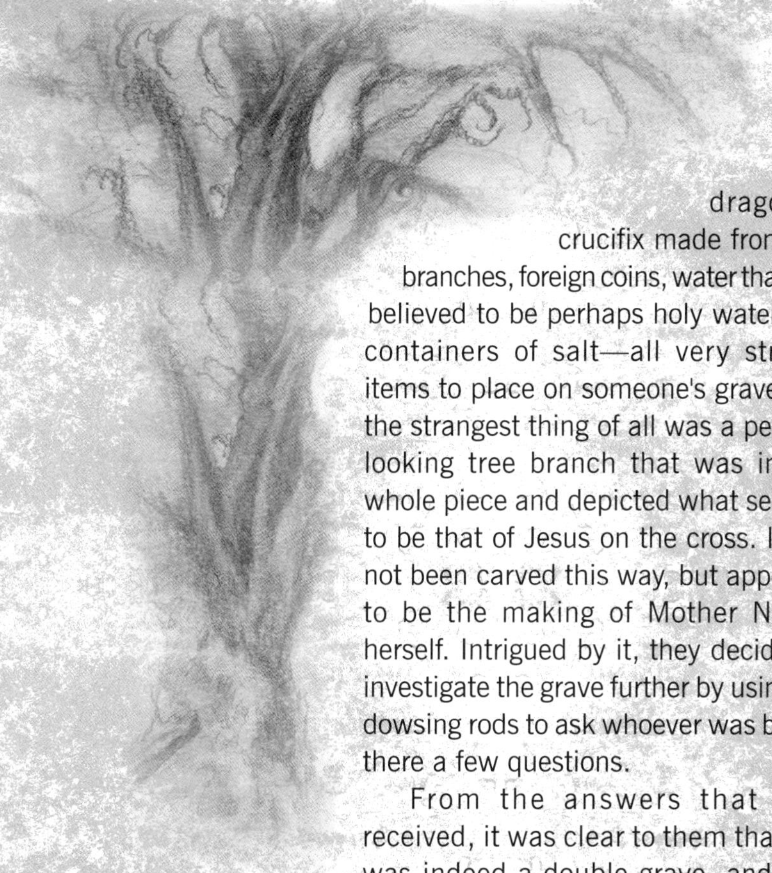

dragon, a crucifix made from two branches, foreign coins, water that they believed to be perhaps holy water, and containers of salt—all very strange items to place on someone's grave. But the strangest thing of all was a peculiar looking tree branch that was in one whole piece and depicted what seemed to be that of Jesus on the cross. It had not been carved this way, but appeared to be the making of Mother Nature herself. Intrigued by it, they decided to investigate the grave further by using the dowsing rods to ask whoever was buried there a few questions.

From the answers that they received, it was clear to them that this was indeed a double grave, and they were communicating with the spirit of the person buried at the top. The entity causing them to feel all the negative feelings was placed underneath. Throughout their time that night in the cemetery, they also unexpectedly contacted the spirit of a deceased Grandmother figure that was buried there. She wanted to communicate with them and she confirmed, through their questions directed to her with the dowsing rods, that two people were buried in this grave. As the dowsing rods were only capable of interpreting simple yes and no answers, the team began to think of questions they were wanting to ask the spirit who was buried at the top of the grave, as *it* would intermittently interrupt their thoughts with his feelings of terror, dread, and despair.

Nancy: "Are you lonely?"
Spirit: *"Yes."*
Nancy: "Do you like it when we come to visit?"
Spirit: *"Yes."*
Nancy: "Do you have visitors other than us?"
Spirit: *"Yes."*
Nancy: "Do friends and family come to visit?"
Spirit: *"Yes."*
Nancy: "Do they come often?"
Spirit: *"No."*

Nancy then focused on the frightened feelings she and the team had been picking up from him.

Nancy: "Are you afraid?"
Spirit: *"Yes."*
Nancy: "Are you scared of the other person in the grave?"
Spirit: *"Yes."*
Nancy: "Do you want to move on?"

The spirit indicated that he did, but that *He*—the other person in the grave with him—won't let him. The spirit said that person was holding him back and he was really scared.

At this point, Nancy and the others could truly feel his terror. They were all feeling this poor spirit's anguish and fear. They knew he was afraid of the entity buried beneath him and who he believed had a great hold over him. *He* could not comprehend how the team could free him and help him to cross over.

The team felt that this evil entity must have done some very terrible things in its life, or perhaps practiced many bad intentions, and they sensed that it had no remorse. Tina stressed how she felt that this entity—or 'thing' as she referred to it—was somehow holding the other spirit hostage and, as long as relatives and friends of the person buried at the top of the grave were visiting and giving it attention, the entity below would not release the spirit so he could cross over successfully to the other side.

Nancy knew they needed additional help from a higher source and asked God for his helping hand with this situation—and, within moments, Nancy was speaking in tongues. This kind of communication usually occurs when a person is in a meditative state and begins to utter an unknown language of which they have no conscious control; it's considered to be conversation with divine angelic beings. There are interpreters who can translate what the person is actually saying, but on this occasion there was no interpreter present, and neither Matthew nor Tina had any idea what Nancy was saying.

Nancy herself had *no* idea of the words she was speaking, but in her mind she knew that she was telling whatever malevolent spirit that was present with them that it could not do to them what it was doing to the spirit that it was holding captive. The team was not going to give this evil entity any power to manipulate them. Furthermore, she told *it* that God was above *it* and that he was the highest supreme being and always in command.

Matthew thought that the best way to deal with this evil malevolent presence was to perform a short exorcism, and being of Catholic faith, he had come prepared with his book of exorcism practices.

However, during Nancy's meditative state, Tina became quite ill with pains to her stomach. The pains became so severe...she could no longer stand. It seemed that this entity waited for an opportune moment when her wall of protection might have weakened and suddenly grasped hold to harm her physically. Tina became so weak that Nancy and Matthew had to support her every move. Matthew could no longer perform the exorcism as Tina was in such excruciating pain, and at one point in the beginning of the exorcism, both Nancy and Matthew thought they heard a growling sound coming from Tina, who had doubled-over. They knew they had done all they could for the spirit at the grave and decided that they had very little option but to leave the cemetery now, so they quickly recited their closing prayer and left..

Still holding on to Tina as they walked towards the perimeter to exit the grounds, they decided that on the count of three they would take a step together over the perimeter. They knew that once they did this, the normality of the outside living world would return.

One... two... three... They were back in the living world and again hearing all the sounds that they couldn't hear while in the cemetery. Dogs barking in the distance, the sound of traffic, the crickets, and the birds—all except for that of the banging sound on the flagpole in the cemetery. Once more the atmosphere became a typical night in the desert. They had exited the cemetery—and the paranormal activity had totally vanished!

Conclusion

As cemeteries are the number one talked about places for ghost hunting along with churches and other old buildings, it's advisable to not pursue a ghost hunt alone, as a whole manner of paranormal occurrences can present themselves. It's important to have professional ghost hunters with you at all times in case an unexpected situation gets out-of-hand.

On the many occasions that LVSSI had visited this cemetery for the specific reason of ghost hunting, they had always experienced some kind of paranormal activity, but for some reason on this particular night it was more intense. It was a full moon after all, and full moons are known to increase supernatural activity. This cemetery is the only one known to them to have a very strange magical barrier to it. The fact that all sounds disappear from the outside of the perimeter and that no insects are to be found on the grounds is quite bizarre.

As for the spirit that needed their help to be freed from the entity buried below it, the team had tried everything in their power to remove its spiritual hold on him many times, but to date have been unsuccessful. They feel sorry and saddened that they have not been able to help him cross over and are uncertain if they will ever be able to. The demonic spirit that lies beneath it is utterly powerful, and even in death, it still possesses malevolent intentions.

Tina experienced severe physical pain from this entity—*a spiritual attack*. She had also noticed three bloody scratch marks on her arm while still in the cemetery, but it was not until she arrived home later that night that she saw three large scratch marks on her back. This was not the first time that she or the team had experienced such a spiritual attack; on previous visits, they have been scratched, prodded, pushed to the ground, their hair has been pulled, and this entity has even tried to choke them. It is very common for people to experience this type of an attack from malevolent spirits and goes to prove that you can never be too safe in any ghost hunt no matter how well prepared you think you might be.

Matthew had researched the records to this grave from the local County and was surprised to discover that there are in fact records of *only* the person buried at the top of the grave, not the person below him. Yet the mound to the grave is high, indicating that two people are buried there. In addition, they had confirmation from the dowsing rods and the spirit of the "Grandmother" that there were indeed two people buried there.

The team had all of their necessary equipment with them that night, which unfortunately yielded little results. Although surprisingly no EVPs were captured, the EMF detectors did show some energy disturbance out there. They also saw what they at first considered to be spirit orbs on their collection of photographs, but as the area was extremely dusty from the desert terrain, they decided that their photographic evidence was inconclusive.

14

Ukulele

Location: *North Las Vegas, Nevada*
Paranormal Activity: *Ukulele Being Played, Whispering, Footsteps, Knocking and Banging, Electrical Problems, and Objects Disappearing and Reappearing*
Investigators: *Tina and Steve Carlson, Nancy Riggs, and Matthew Winn*

Resident ghost plays Ukulele! Doesn't that statement grab your attention—and it sure caught the owners' attention when they began hearing its strings frequently being plucked throughout the day and night. As I have said in previous chapters, ghosts will try anything to get your attention, and if it means communicating through the form of a musical instrument, believe me they will!

If you live within the City of Las Vegas and happen to see a black SUV with "GOT GHOST" written on the rear view window, that's Tina Carlson's vehicle. This is one of the ways that LVSSI advertises its ghost investigation services, and over the years, they have had many people inquire as to what GOT GHOST is all about. Mr. Martinez was one of those people who saw the advertisement on Tina's vehicle and called her one day in 2007 to ask if LVSSI could pay a visit to his family's home...as he believed that they did indeed GOT GHOST.

He, his wife, and three children lived in a two-story house, approximately six years old, in an upscale part of the neighborhood. Although it was Mr. Martinez who initially began experiencing the paranormal occurrences, his two sons, aged six and eleven, and his nine-year-old daughter had also started to experience the strange activity for themselves and it reached a point where they were becoming increasingly upset and bothered by it.

His daughter, Elizabeth, would talk about how she was seeing shadow people in her bedroom—and one of them had reached out to touch her as she lay in bed one night. She now refused to sleep in her room because of it. The television in the boys' bedroom frequently switched on all by itself, scaring them both to no end, and they would end up sleeping with their parents for the night whenever it happened.

There was much paranormal activity in their home: Odors of perfume, flowers, sulfur, excrement, and food would just manifest from nowhere and then disappear from where it came; footsteps and frequent knocking and banging was heard without any obvious source, along with disembodied voices that were heard sometimes whispering, crying, yelling, and speaking the occasional word. Objects disappearing and reappearing was nothing new to the family, as well as the shocking movement of Mr. and Mrs. Martinez' bed all by itself on several occasions.

They also would constantly find electrical appliances operating on their own accord or malfunction suddenly for no particular reason, along with light bulbs burning out with unusual frequency and the doorbell ringing periodically all by itself. These are all very usual and common phenomena in the paranormal realm and the list of odd goings-on in this home is quite long. Not only were these occurrences bothering the family, they were also affecting their German shepherd...as their resident spirit would often and suddenly lash out to hit it.

But the most bizarre—and scariest of all—activity that they experienced was to *hear and physically see* the strings being strummed on their ukulele by an unknown presence no matter whether it was day or night. The instrument happened to be in Elizabeth's bedroom sitting on her dresser, and as the interference of paranormal activity had now reached its peak, the Martinez family could no longer deal with the nonsense. Mr. Martinez arranged for LVSSI to visit their home and see how they could help rid them of the ghostly phenomena.

When LVSSI arrived, Mr. Martinez did most of the talking with them, as his wife did not speak much English. They were a very religious Spanish family and could not understand what was going on in their home. It was all too much for them to cope with, especially for their young children. He explained to Tina how he had previously used sage to cleanse the house, but the paranormal activity still continued to dominate it! Tina, as the main investigator, always sits and talks with the family before LVSSI begins their investigation. Not only does she take notes of the kinds of phenomena the family is experiencing, she also explains that prior to cleansing the home they, LVSSI, always gives the spirit a choice to move on. If the spirit doesn't like what it finds when it crosses over to the spirit world, it can then return to this plane of existence, but *not* to this particular house.

Once a spirit has crossed over, it doesn't usually decide to come back to this earthly plane. Spirits are, in fact, no different from living human beings in that they are not in favor of being bossed around and told what to do. The investigators will help coax a spirit to move on in order for it to be settled and at peace in the spirit realm where it belongs, but some spirits might still possess the strong persona it once had on the earthly plane and long to come back for reasons that are unclear to the owner of the home.

As the team had now started to wander around the house, it was not long before they tuned into the presence of paranormal activity and picking up the vibes of which rooms to explore first. Tina wandered around the upstairs hallway, Nancy checked out one of the bedrooms, Steve set up their equipment in a different room, and Matthew began to investigate Elizabeth's bedroom. Within moments, Matthew shouted to Tina to come into Elizabeth's room—there sitting on the back of the dresser and leaning against the wall was the ukulele...with its strings mysteriously being plucked!

They both heard the pluck, pluck, pluck sound loud and clear and were shocked to actually *see* the strings on this instrument clearly being played all by itself. Nancy came into the room shortly afterwards to see what was going on and could not believe what she was witnessing. Though they were all initially left speechless at what they were all seeing, they began to investigate what could possibly be making the strings move like this; they checked all around the instrument, feeling if any vibration was coming from the opposite side of the wall. The ukulele now suddenly stopped playing. They all stepped back and held their breath in anticipation of what was to follow... Low and behold, it started to play once again.

Nancy took a reading of the room temperature, which did, in fact, show signs of a considerable decrease in temperature as the ukulele was being played. They also took photographs and used both of their video and audio recorders to try and collect as much evidence as they could. They checked to see if the culprit was the air conditioning—that perhaps its vibrating through the wall was making the strings move—asked the family to switch it off for a few moments while they checked it. But it didn't seem to make any difference as the ukulele's strings would stop and then start to play all over again. They took it off the dresser and laid it flat on the floor, but again, within a few seconds, it started to play. It just continued to repeatedly play no matter what the team did to try and stop it.

They even placed it in various parts of the room to see if it would make any difference and they could feel the vibration of the strings actually being plucked as they placed their hands on it, but nothing stopped it from playing. Steve eventually came into the room from having set up equipment in other locations of the house. Told what had just happened and, as the skeptical investigator among them, he decided to carry out further experiments in order to try and find answers for himself.

He walked around the room to see if there was any vibration coming from the floor boards and the walls, even asking the owners, once again, to switch off the air conditioning so that he could check all the air vents and that air wasn't blowing on the strings. He went through every logical and illogical possibility, even as far as stomping outside the bedroom, and heavily walking around in the very next room. He also went outside to the window to see if there was any breeze that might be blowing through, but he was at a loss to find any answers as to why or what could possibly be making this instrument play. He ultimately realized that this was indeed a genuine paranormal phenomenon. They had done everything in their power to find out what might be interfering with it, but there were no obvious signs.

As the ukulele had now become silent once again, the team decided that the next room to investigate was the boys' bedroom. It was a typical boys' room with toys and games strewn about, as well as a television and even a pet gerbil, but the team *felt* a definite heaviness in this room. Matthew thought it was now time to get out the dowsing rods to see if he could make contact with any presence that might be lingering in there, but as soon as he did, the rods started spinning like the blades of a helicopter, each in a different direction. They wouldn't stay straight no matter how much Matthew tried to stop them.

Amused and somewhat curious at what was happening with Matthew's rods, Nancy took out her dowsing rods to see what hers might do. Low and behold her set of rods started to do the exact same thing. Tina, as an empathic, uses only her feelings for guidance. She rarely uses the dowsing rods for answers to any ghostly situation, but she, too, was curious to see what would happen if another set of rods was used. As she took a set from the bag, sure enough... the exact same thing happened all over again. Now all three sets of dowsing rods were spinning out of control, periodically stopping to reverse their direction. The team even turned them to a different angle to see if that made a difference, but the rods still spun in all directions. No matter what questions the team asked the spirit in this room, there were never any answers given—the rods just kept spinning out of control. They stayed in the boys' bedroom for forty-five minutes testing the rods, but were at a loss as to why they were behaving in such a manner.

Soon enough, though, they were all laughing uncontrollably, as they had never experienced anything like this before. Steve knocked on the door and asked what was happening in there as everyone was laughing so loud. Steve was also totally perplexed to see all of these sets of dowsing rods spinning out of control and knew that the rods were definitely picking up on some very strange and intense energy.

After a short while, they moved on to the master bedroom. Matthew walked over to the bed and sat down, looking around the room to see if he could tune in to any ghostly presence that might be in there. Tina sat on the floor by the wall with her legs out stretched, trying to also tune in to what might be present, while Nancy began taking random photographs around the room. This was the bedroom of Mr. and Mrs. Martinez who had experienced their bed moving on many occasions. Suddenly, a loud 'clunk' was heard where Tina was sitting. It was a sound similar to that of someone kicking a wall. Nancy immediately turned her camera to the spot where the sound was heard, but it was not until the photographs were later developed that one of them showed a very bright orb moving above the top of Tina's leg. Figures of shadow people were also frequently seen in the bedroom mirrors, and the owners would catch glimpses of them in the master bathroom through the corner of their eyes. This would quite often concern Mrs. Martinez more than her husband, who appeared to be a little more laid back about the ghostly interaction.

During the latter part of the investigation, a Christian group from the family's church showed up at their home for a meeting. Mr. Martinez had completely forgotten that he had arranged for the church group to meet at the house at the same time he had LVSSI to investigate his property, and apologized profusely to both groups for the genuine mistake. However, the religious group quickly became very uncomfortable with the situation of why LVSSI was there and decided that they would wait outside the house while the team finished their investigation and the cleansing.

In a fairly large sized home such as this one, a cleansing can take up to fifty minutes or so—and LVSSI is very thorough with their final cleansing as no space is left *un-cleansed*. Cupboards, closets, under beds, even inside drawers, and shower stalls are all given the utmost attention during the process, so that there is never a place left for a spirit to hide. However in some instances, although a complete cleansing has taken place with the necessary use of herbs and prayer, a spirit can still possess strong intentions to return to that particular residency and that is exactly what happened at the Martinez home. Within a couple of weeks, the team had to return a second time to repeat the cleansing process, and rid the spirit's presence from their home once and for all.

Conclusion

Never under estimate a spirit's ability of how it might choose to make contact with you. If various other methods of contact by a spirit does not seem to attract your attention at first, going one step further to use a musical instrument just might be the next plan of action for them.

During the team's investigation of the Martinez home, they were never able to find out if the spirit present was that of a male or female and whether it was a deceased relative just visiting the family or even possibly a wandering spirit. But although the presence of it felt by them was one with no bad intentions, they did sense it to be anxious and somewhat mischievous. Even if it had been connected to the family, usually Tina can feel it immediately, but this time it was very much a sense of a neutral presence.

It was also discovered during the investigation that there were some underlying emotional family issues present within the home—and any high emotional energy can most definitely attract a spirit into your space, and will stay regardless of what you might try to do to remove it. Maybe this was the real reason that the spirit found its way into the Martinez home...because of the emotional upset.

Although LVSSI had taken footage of the ukulele mysteriously being played, it did not show the action of the strings on the film itself. But they did capture an audio recording of the instrument being played. Even though the family had experienced the whispering, crying, and yelling sounds from the spirit, strangely enough no EVPs were captured at that time. The only real positive proof that they had experienced the spirit being present was through the dowsing rods reacting in a very unusual manner when they were investigating the boys' bedroom.

15

The Asian Man

Location: *Central Las Vegas, Nevada*
Paranormal Activity: *Strange Noises, Footsteps, Knocking Sounds, Electrical Problems, and Whispering*
Investigator: *Matthew Winn*

Imagine the scary thought for a moment of being locked in a room in your home by a ghost! A most frightening experience for anyone to encounter, and although it sounds quite unbelievable, that is exactly what happened in this next investigation that scared one of the residents to their core.

Greg and Tim are two friends in their twenties who share an apartment together in Central Las Vegas. They had only lived in their apartment for a short period of six months when the paranormal phenomena started to interrupt their daily lives. Actually, the first month of living in their apartment was ghost free, but then unexpectedly various signs of some *other presence* sharing their space became very evident to them. All of the pieces started to quickly come together—mysterious footsteps throughout the apartment, whispering sounds, the strange noises and knocking sounds that they frequently heard, plus the repeated electrical problems that often occurred made Tim and Greg realize that they were not alone—they had a ghost!

While most of the strange occurrences happened mainly during the late evenings, it would also manifest throughout the day—sometimes daily, sometimes weekly; but certainly always on a regular basis. Their pet cats were also affected by the activity, displaying very strange behavior whenever the supernatural showed its presence. They often came running out of one of the rooms with their fur literally standing up on end, and made growling sounds whenever the unseen presence was hanging around. Not to mention scratching at the walls and staring at what appeared to be nothing in the middle of the room.

Animals are so sensitive and finely in tune to any strange energy that is not immediately sensed by humans. Dogs, cats, and even birds can easily pick up on any unusual energy and unwelcome entities, but cats most especially tend to be the more intuitive of the species, knowing when something strange and out of sorts is occupying their domain.

Greg and Tim were feeling pretty anxious, frightened, and confused about the apartment being haunted. Greg, who was a good friend of Matthew's and knew of his involvement with LVSSI, called him to ask if he could investigate the situation. The paranormal activity had increased and was becoming much more intense. It was to the point where the ghost was now targeting Greg...even locking him in one of the rooms in his apartment. He was also having repeated nightmares of a strange looking Asian man that followed him around—his eyes would turn red—before he disappeared.

When Matthew arrived at Greg and Tim's apartment, it was Tim who met and spoke with Matthew as Greg was not home that evening. He explained about all of the weird circumstances that had occurred during the five months of them living in, adding that the ghost seemed to now be focusing more on Greg by giving him nightmares and even locking him in a room. Sometimes they would discover that doors previously locked had become mysteriously unlocked and vice versa. They have even seen the *apparition* of this Asian man a number of times throughout their apartment.

Although the ghost appeared pretty much as a shadow figure, they could clearly see his strong Asian features, and while they felt the spirit was frightening but *not threatening*, they, nevertheless, wanted it removed from their home.

As Matthew began investigating the apartment, he started taking a number of photographs, pointing the camera anywhere in the room that he felt he should intuitively point it. He also took a series of both temperature and EMF readings throughout the rooms, which showed several unexplainable high-energy fluctuations in a number of places. No hot or cold spots seemed to be present that night, and although Greg and Tim had frequently heard low whispering sounds, surprisingly there were no EVPs captured during Matthew's time at the apartment.

At Greg and Tim's request, a *cleansing* of their home was performed, as the final part of the investigation. Using both salt and sage, accompanied by sacred prayers, Matthew performed the cleansing throughout the apartment. After a week passed, Matthew contacted them to see if all was quiet and if the ghostly activity had now ceased. He was happy to hear the positive news that things had now returned to normal for his friends...just as it was when they had first moved into their apartment. The cats had also now settled back to their normal selves and their strange behavior had stopped once and for all.

Conclusion

Although this case was pretty straightforward, it was never concluded *why* the spirit of the Asian man targeted only Greg in this haunting. Matthew could not conclude to any viable explanation for it. Perhaps the spirit was in fact a wandering spirit, or maybe a previous resident who had once lived—and died—in their apartment and he wanted to let them know that it was still his home. Any one of these explanations could be possible.

Although both Tim and especially Greg had not had any physical contact with this spirit, he most definitely wanted to communicate and let his presence be known by behaving mischievously, including by locking Greg in one of the rooms on many occasions. Not to mention the recurring nightmares of the Asian man showing up in Greg's dreams. As it has been stated in many of the previous cases, spirits can contact you in many ways—and appearing in your dreams is just another form of communication that they find so easy to do.

Photographs later developed revealed a number of orb phenomena in them, as well as high-energy fluctuations shown on the EMF meters throughout Matthew's investigation. Surprisingly there were no EVPs captured that night and no video footage of any unusual activity, nor the presence of the Asian man himself.

KESARA

16

Beloved Brother

Location: *Sahara / Decatur area, Las Vegas, Nevada*
Paranormal Activity: *Spirit Calling Out Names, Shadow People, Spirit Trying to Physically Touch, Messages on the Mirror, Small Dark Shadows, and Footsteps*
Investigators: *Tina Carlson, Nancy Riggs, and Matthew Winn*

Strange as it may be, sometimes a pregnancy can invoke a myriad of ghost activity in the home, and this next case is a perfect example of that and of how a haunting manifested between three family households...to the point where they were all experiencing the same paranormal events.

Gail Manning is a young mother in her early twenties who, during her two pregnancies, experienced ghost activity in her home. Gail and her husband Grant had lived in the same apartment throughout both of Gail's pregnancies, and during her very first one a couple of years ago, they witnessed a host of strange and unusual activity that they could only attribute to as ghost related. The phenomena manifested for a few months into

Gail's pregnancy, but then disappeared some months prior to their daughter being born.

During Gail's second pregnancy with her son, the ghost activity resumed again, but to the point where it increased and intensified throughout the whole nine months of carrying her baby. After her son was born, the paranormal occurrences seemed to subside but were still fairly active, just not as active as when she had been pregnant. It was only a couple of weeks after the baby was born that Gail contacted Tina at LVSSI, as she and Grant were extremely curious as to why this activity would occupy their apartment on both occasions of her being pregnant.

Tina and Nancy met with Gail for a preliminary meeting one evening that lasted for two full hours. Gail was very curious and intrigued about her ghost situation and had so many questions to ask. During the course of the evening, she described how she had been seeing movement out of the corner of her eye—in particular she was seeing a dark, shadowy silhouette leaning over her baby's crib. Her two-year-old daughter was also scared from seeing it and would not sleep alone in her bedroom.

Gail recalled how one night as her husband awoke, he happened to glance across to the crib and *saw* the same black shadowy figure leaning over it, which shocked and scared him to no end. On several occasions, always at night, he heard a voice calling out *daddy*, but when he would check on his two-year-old daughter thinking that it was she who was calling out, she'd be fast asleep. Grant had another older daughter, from a previous marriage, who would visit and stay with them sometimes, and she too heard the word *daddy* being called out. And often, when Grant worked at his computer, he would see this shadow person standing in the hallway; he also occasionally had the feeling of someone reaching out to touch him when he would be taking a shower, but could never see the physical presence of anyone.

Gail was given a beautiful large, wood-framed mirror, by a family member, that had been handed down to her as a precious heirloom, and to her surprise, she frequently saw a shadow person walking past it. Her two-year-old daughter would also see it, and even the newborn baby would turn his head whenever he caught sight of the strange dark figure walking by.

Gail also happened to see on a number of occasions small dark shadows running up and down the hallway, hearing their footsteps, as they ran back and forth.

Gail told Tina and Nancy that she had her suspicions of who she thought this shadow person might be, but did not want to reveal it to them that night. She explained that she wanted LVSSI to investigate it for themselves, and of course, the team was eager to explore the situation and find out who exactly was haunting her apartment.

During the meeting, Gail revealed to Tina and Nancy how she thought that she herself had some psychic ability. She recalled a strange incident that had happened during a trip to the famous Whaley House in California, which has a reputation of being extremely haunted, explaining that as she was walking down the backstairs of the building, she felt an irritation around her neck and noticed that she had mysteriously developed a rope burn there. Although Gail had heard rumors that the building was in fact haunted, she had no prior knowledge of the history of the Whaley House, but later found out that a series of hangings had actually taken place in the exact location of where Gail had been visiting. Tina and Nancy agreed that this was a sign that she did seem to show some intuitive ability, especially as her body had experienced physical impressions from the hangings in that location.

As the evening's meeting came to a close, Tina and Nancy made arrangements for the team to visit Gail's apartment to carry out their investigation of her on-going paranormal activity. Once arriving at her home a week later, they began their investigation by asking to be shown around the various rooms where the phenomenon was being experienced. As Gail showed them around, Tina felt a distinct feeling that every room did actually have some kind of paranormal activity in it, but sensed the strongest feeling of a presence in the master bedroom.

Setting up their equipment in there, they took the EMF detector and placed it in the middle of the bed—and it immediately lit up! This confirmed to them the strong sense of a presence...that they were definitely not alone, but they wanted to experiment with the EMF meter to see if it would light up in other places around the room. They held it up to the ceiling close to the air vents to see if there was any interference coming directly from the airflow that could possibly be making it light up, but it did not. They also placed it directly underneath the bed, but it still did not light up. Yet, strangely, the very moment they placed the meter back onto the bed...it lit up right away.

Another piece of equipment they used was the cell sensor, which also monitors the electro-magnetic field in the room and beeps whenever it picks up fluctuations of unknown energy in the environment. The monitor on this device was showing quite a high, active reading, reaching mid-range levels that were beyond the normal range of detecting electro-magnetic fields. Most of the teams' equipment that night was divided between both the master bedroom and the daughter's bedroom, but Tina instinctively knew that the master bedroom would show signs of the strongest paranormal presence.

At first Tina felt that the spirit was standing back, not wanting to come forward and communicate with them. She began to tune in to its presence and picked up information that it was a male in his early twenties, and, when he was alive, he had been somewhat knowledgeable and interested in such things as ghost hunting. This male entity proved this by giving Tina various signals throughout the investigation.

Meanwhile, the strong presence of this entity began to physically affect Nancy, making her feel nauseous and very dizzy. She also felt sudden pains in her chest and had to sit for a while until she felt like her normal self. In fact they were all physically affected in some way by its presence, but after a few moments, they felt well enough to continue with the investigation.

Matthew decided to use the dowsing rods to see what information he could pick up directly from the spirit. As he held them in place, one of the questions Tina asked the spirit was if he was a family member; the rods crossed immediately, giving a positive reply. She had the distinct impression that he didn't stay in the apartment permanently, but moved around from one family member to another—particularly on Gail's husband's side of the family.

After experiencing strong paranormal activity for a full hour in the master bedroom, including that of seeing a number of orbs passing through the room, they continued with their investigation in Gail's daughter's room. They had switched some of their equipment around from the master bedroom to the child's room, but just as soon as they had done this, the motion detector started to sense movement back in the master bedroom. The cell sensor that was placed on the bed was now beeping erratically, showing signs that a presence was in there, and whenever they asked a question to the spirit of where he actually was, *he* communicated back to them by having the dowsing rods point directly towards the master bedroom.

Even though Gail's two-year-old daughter was afraid to sleep in her bedroom as she had experienced a few strange things, there appeared to be very little paranormal activity in there that night. However, the team did experience seeing orb phenomena in this room throughout the time of their investigation, but it was apparent to them that this spirit moved from room to room in the apartment. Once again Tina was getting a strong feeling that this male spirit definitely knew something about ghost hunting; the spirit even conveyed somewhat of a humorous message to her that the team needed to prove his presence and he was not going to give them any clues as to his whereabouts! It was evident to them that he was clearly making the statement that if indeed the team were confident ghost hunters, then they would have to prove that they knew where to seek him out!

Starting precisely at 10:01 p.m., the paranormal activity became abundant in the master bedroom; a flurry of events escalated and continued non-stop for a full thirty minutes. The motion detector alone had responded twenty-one times in total and the cell sensor reacted six times throughout the duration of this activity. As the team stood watching through the cameras from the child's bedroom, they meticulously timed each individual occurrence as it happened, noticing that it would sometimes take the spirit a little longer to regain the energy it needed in order to re-activate the devices in between each piece of equipment beeping or lighting up. At the time Nancy was holding the remote viewer device, which showed no visible sign of a presence walking in front of the camera. No matter where the motion detector was pointed in the master bedroom, the remote viewer camera was also focused in that same direction and would have clearly shown any physical motion detected should there have been any.

Suddenly, to everyone's surprise, the paranormal activity came to an abrupt stop—and the team was left with the feeling that the spirit had totally disappeared. It seemed that the spirit had made the decision to end the night's investigation; all that now remained was for the team to pack away their equipment and for Tina to brief Gail on what they had experienced throughout the night, but would give her a more detailed analysis once they had completed the full evidence report.

"Correct me if I'm wrong," Tina said to Gail, "but we feel that the spirit haunting your apartment is a male in his early twenties, of a slight physical build, and a good sense of humor. He's definitely a family member, but he doesn't stay here; he frequently visits you and two other family members, his siblings, and his parents."

Gail was stunned to hear what Tina was saying. She admitted that Tina was, in fact, extremely accurate in her perceptions and information of the spirit's activity—and that *he* does indeed visit other family members on her husband's side of the family. Grant's two other brothers had both experienced the same paranormal happenings as she and Grant.

Gail began to reveal that she had known all along who she suspected this spirit to be—her husband's brother who, in his early twenties, had been killed unexpectedly in a car accident many years earlier. Whenever there was news of a pregnancy in the family and especially that of a boy about to be born, they would always experience an abundance of paranormal occurrences in their homes. What also seemed to enhance the on-going ghostly behavior was that Grant and his other brothers had all named their newborn sons in honor of their deceased beloved brother.

As it was now confirmed to Gail and Grant that the spirit visiting them was a family member, they chose not to go through with a cleansing to remove him from their home. However, Gail did request that the team convey a message to him and ask that he please stop frightening the children and not to appear in their daughter's bedroom anymore. Tina acknowledged Gail's request and relayed the message to him. She also told Gail that if ever she felt that he was causing a disturbance in the apartment, she should simply address him by his name and tell him that he needs to stop the activity, or he could no longer visit their home.

After a couple of weeks had passed since the investigation, Gail contacted Tina to let her know that although the spirit was still visiting their apartment, he was no longer scaring the children and that things had become much more peaceful and settled in their home. She and Grant were extremely happy with the outcome of LVSSI's investigation, and that Grant's brother's spirit was no longer haunting their apartment so intensely as he had been doing previously.

Conclusion

There are no logical explanations as to why a pregnancy would invoke paranormal manifestations, but in this particular ghost case, the spirit felt the need to convey his extreme happiness to his three family members in knowing of their individual pregnancies, and most especially that they were naming their three newborn sons after him. It's not unusual for a spirit to visit more than one family member, but what was interesting about this case was that he repeated the exact paranormal behavior to all of his siblings throughout their pregnancies.

Although the main focus of the investigation was in the master bedroom and the daughter's bedroom, at one point they felt an urge to extend their investigation into the master bathroom. In here Nancy had experienced the distinct smell of smoke, and although the door to the toilet was initially closed, she could see from the corner of her eye that it was gradually opening a good few inches or more.

A series of photographs were taken in the master bathroom that night, as well as in other rooms, but it was not until they were later developed that one photo in particular, taken by Matthew, revealed a number "3" written in one corner of the vanity mirror in the bathroom. In the other corner was written the word "HA HA," and appeared to have been written as a smear on the glass in a strange 'foggy' type of writing. Other photographs that Tina had later taken in the bathroom showed that the writing had mysteriously disappeared as quickly as it had appeared. There had been no one in the bathroom throughout the whole evening prior to them investigating it. Grant and his two-year-old daughter were not home, and Gail and her baby had been sitting downstairs throughout the entire investigation.

It appears evident that the spirit was communicating to them through the use of various devices that night; the EMF detector, the Cell Sensor, cameras, dowsing rods, and especially through his capability of writing on the vanity mirror. I don't think that it's a far stretch of the imagination to say that the number '3' represented the three new additions to the family that were all named after him, and as he had a good sense of humor and a playful personality, he wrote the word "HA HA" to prove the point.

During his strong presence in the master bedroom, which caused Nancy to feel quite ill, she thought this to be his way of interacting with her, by manifesting the pains in her chest to represent the force of the steering wheel as it hit him hard against his upper body at the time of his unexpected and untimely death. Of course LVSSI had no idea how he had died until the investigation was over and Gail revealed the details of his sudden passing.

As for the small dark shadows that Gail had seen running up and down the hallway, Tina came to the conclusion that what Gail had actually been experiencing was something called residual energy. Although a little difficult to understand, this type of energy is often left behind in the home from previous residents; an energy that the home has held as a memory, a 'recording' that continues to play itself over and over. Tina sensed that this had been the energy from young children who had lived in the apartment prior to Gail and Grant moving in and it was their residual energy that the apartment was processing. This is a very common type of haunting. Residual energy doesn't really interact with people as such, but shows itself when the conditions happen to be just right.

17

The Talking Telephone

Location: *Charleston / Rancho Area, Las Vegas, Nevada*
Paranormal Activity: *Voice Speaking through Child's Toy Telephone, Whispering, Footsteps, and Shadow People*
Investigators: *Tina Carlson and Nancy Riggs*

As I had previously stated in the Introduction, telephones are a very popular form of communication for a ghost wanting to talk to you, and in this ghost investigation, even a child's toy telephone was used by the ghost to communicate to one of the residents.

When Gloria and her family moved into their house seven years ago, they had only lived there for a couple of weeks when Gloria first began to sense a negative presence of something in the home. Her three children ages seventeen, four, and two, were also aware of the strange, unseen presence that would occupy their home during most of the days and nights. Because of this, they would keep all of their televisions switched on twenty-four hours a day, seven days a week to block out what they were experiencing and felt much safer doing this. Gloria's sixty-three-year-old mother also lived with them on the upper level of the two-story house, while her ex-husband's parents lived downstairs in the property.

Among the myriad of paranormal activity dwelling in their home, shadow people had been seen often lingering in the hallway, along with footsteps, voices, and whispering that was heard by all of the family members. On one particular day, they even witnessed a loaf of bread being knocked off the top of the refrigerator—it flew across the kitchen and into the dining room that was a good fifteen feet away. Shocked at what they had seen, Gloria knew at that point that her sense and observations of things not being quite right in the home was real...and that she was *NOT* going crazy. She concluded that the presence of a ghost was the only explanation for all of the strange and recurring activity.

LVSSI was soon contacted by Gloria, who located them via the Internet, as the ghost activity had now escalated over the couple of months prior to Gloria contacting them. After a preliminary meeting had taken place, both Tina and Nancy arrived at the house around eight o'clock that particular night to carry out the investigation. They toured the property with Gloria, who informed them that most of the activity would happen in the children's bedrooms and that her four-year-old daughter has been seen having conversations with whoever or whatever was present.

"Hi, my name's Olivia," she would say, as she made eye contact with whoever was there, followed by the occasional nod of the head and a yes or a no answer to questions that the ghost was presumably asking her. She would follow and talk to it as it moved around the room, and would even randomly answer to the ghost, "Yes, Grandma's doing fine."

Tina decided to start the investigation in this particular bedroom, the smallest of the children's rooms. Nancy took a temperature reading that showed it to be eighty-six degrees, fairly warm. But there was nothing really abnormal in here, except for the fact that Nancy almost immediately started to feel pressure in her head, which was always a sure sign to her that an unseen presence was close by. However, no communication was attempted by spirit at that time. Tina switched off the lights and took a series of photographs wherever she felt an intuitive sense to point the camera. Although they stayed in this room for approximately twenty minutes or so, no paranormal activity presented itself, so they moved on into the seventeen-year-old daughter's bedroom.

The temperature in this room read the same as the previous one, eighty-six degrees, and once again Nancy started to feel dizzy and somewhat unsteady on her feet. She had to hold onto a chair while trying to regain her balance. It seemed evident that the spirit was sharing Nancy's space and had followed them both into the bedroom, but the strange thing was that there was no sign of a drop in temperature, which is usually a positive indicator for a spirit suddenly being present. Tina again took random photographs while the lights were switched off, and she and Nancy stayed in this room for a period of twenty-five minutes.

This bedroom belonged to Gloria's oldest daughter, who told the investigators that she had an interest in the paranormal. She also told them of an extremely weird incident that she and her friend had experienced in the house one day. As they sat in the living room having a conversation with each other, they were suddenly shocked to hear a voice begin to talk to them from a toy telephone belonging to the younger sister.

"Hello, is anyone there?"

the voice would say, and then repeated itself,

"Hello, is anyone there?"

The strange thing was that this telephone was literally a child's toy, and had no built in electronic mechanism. It had no talking function whatsoever, but would just simply ring a few times to amuse the children once the numbers had been pushed. She explained that this had happened on a couple of occasions, and how she was shocked to discover that a spirit could actually manipulate such a toy in this way. Although somewhat a little scared by it, at the same time she was also intrigued by the spirit's capability.

The master bedroom was the next room of interest, and in here Nancy started to use the dowsing rods to see if the spirit was present, and if so, would it come forward to communicate with her? This time she was in luck. The rods began responding to her every question, with them crossing over each other for a positive answer or opening apart for a negative one. This wasn't the only device that the spirit used to communicate with Nancy, as she also happened to have a small pen light in the upper pocket of her shirt. Every time she asked a question to the spirit, not only would the rods react, but the light at the end of the pen would also flash as well!

The spirit's communication appeared to be in full force while they were investigating this room, as not only were the dowsing rods and the pen light evidence of a presence, but both the cell sensor and the EMF meter were also beeping and responding to the spirit's energy. And yet... it seemed to be unwilling and uncooperative to announce whether it was male or female. It was also very difficult to acquire any photographic evidence in here due to the many reflective surfaces such as mirrors and framed artwork that Gloria had in the room; any photographs taken could have revealed a false and questionable image on them, and so they had to disregard all photographs taken in there.

After investigating both the living room and the kitchen area, which proved to be unsuccessful in showing any signs of paranormal activity, Tina and Nancy decided that they should move on towards the second level of the house, where Gloria's ex-husband's parents lived. They couldn't actually enter the downstairs level as it was securely blocked off with a large piece of plywood, but if Gloria or her in-laws so wished, they could easily remove it should they ever decide to open up that level and make it a larger space again.

Tina felt the urge to place her hand on the plywood and immediately felt that it was being pushed back, or as she put it, that it felt as though it was 'breathing' in some strange way. There was also a sudden drop in temperature in this location that they could not explain, as the whole house was reading a steady eighty-six degrees. Nancy began to feel an uncomfortable pressure to her head once again, which lasted for the duration of her being in this area, and she and Tina came to the conclusion that perhaps the spirit mainly stayed on the downstairs level with Gloria's in-laws.

The unfortunate circumstance was that there were somewhat negative emotions between Gloria and her in-laws and they very rarely spoke to one another, which proved to be fairly awkward for Gloria to approach them with any curious questions of possible ghost experiences that they might have had. Because of this, LVSSI could not fully investigate the lower level of the property, and as they had now completed their investigation of her home, they asked Gloria if she would like for them to perform a house cleansing...to which she eagerly agreed. On this occasion, the team used the herb sweet grass instead of the usual sage, as Gloria's mother had an asthma condition and they did not want the cleansing to affect her breathing in any negative way.

As the team went from room to room asking the spirit to leave the home, a series of prayers, salt, and sweet grass were used in the cleansing ritual. As they approached the front door to cleanse around it, they physically felt a sudden *whoosh*...as the spirit quickly glided passed them and left the house.

LVSSI contacted Gloria a week or so later with the final analysis of their findings, and as she thanked them for their help, she reported that all of the paranormal activity had now completely stopped.

Conclusion

Throughout the investigation of this ghost case, Tina had concluded, through her own sensing and empathic ability, that the spirit was not that belonging to any family member, but in fact a wandering type that had found its way into the house. Gloria had initially felt that there were three separate ghosts in the home, as she attributed certain paranormal activity with one particular ghost and another paranormal occurrence with a different entity, but this was not the case.

Although Nancy used the dowsing rods in all of the bedrooms, she only received a response from them in the master bedroom. Throughout the entire evening, the spirit was totally uncooperative during the use of the dowsing rods, and as Tina points out, sometimes spirits are unsure how to deal with LVSSI being there to investigate a home. For that reason, they always ask the family not to talk about them before they arrive, as this can encourage the spirit to stop its activity completely, or either encourage them to intensify their behavior.

During the night's investigation, no recording device was used to capture any EVPs, as the home environment was much too noisy due to Gloria's two young children being there, and the team would not have been able to capture any genuine unknown voice phenomena on the tape recorder. All photographs were disregarded from this investigation as Gloria was a smoker, and the team did not want to accidentally capture any smoke trails that may have been misidentified as some kind of strange phenomena.

RESARA

18

Ghosts At Boulder Dam Hotel!

Location: *City of Boulder, Nevada*
Paranormal Activity: *A Shadow Person, Knocking on Hotel Room Doors, Bed Covers Being Lifted Off Guests While Sleeping, Lights Being Switched on By Themselves, and Orb Phenomena*
Investigators: *Tina and Steve Carlson, Nancy Riggs, Matthew Winn, and Several LVSSI Trainees*

There are a number of alleged haunted hotels throughout the state of Nevada, and the Boulder Dam Hotel is one of them that LVSSI investigated a few years ago. After hearing reports of various paranormal occurrences at this beautiful historic hotel, LVSSI was eager to perform an investigation there and contacted the owners to arrange a visit. This is their experience...

Boulder Dam Hotel is one of the oldest hotels in the City of Boulder, Nevada. It was built in 1933 to accommodate a large number of tourists who wanted to visit Boulder Dam, which was called Hoover Dam at that time. The hotel is a beautiful two-story Dutch

Colonial building, small in size with a total of thirty-two rooms, but very rich in history. There were a number of famous people of the time who visited the hotel such as; Bette Davis, Shirley Temple, and Will Rogers to name but a few, and as LVSSI had heard that the hotel was haunted, they made an inquiry to ask if they could investigate it.

As it turned out, their ghost inquiry intrigued the hotel owners very much as they to were aware that paranormal activity had been reported on many occasions by a number of visitors who had stayed there over the years, so they openly invited LVSSI to perform an investigation of the building. As the team arrived at the hotel and walked into the foyer, they noticed the original, old-fashion counter that still happened to be used as the registration desk, not to mention the very noticeable old musty smell that accompanied the aged surroundings of the foyer. It made them feel as though they were entering some kind of time warp back to 1933.

The lady at the desk acknowledged their arrival and quickly arranged for someone to cover her position, as she would be their tour guide and showed them around the various rooms of the hotel where all of the paranormal activity had happened. Their first area of investigation was at the upstairs level, where there were two rooms of specific interest that had shown a certain amount of past paranormal activity, and the guide took the team into one of the guest rooms. She began telling them how every time the maid came into this particular room to make the bed, as soon as she went out into the hallway to get something from her housekeeping cart, she'd come back into the room to discover an imprint of someone having just sat on the bed!

As the team had brought along most of their investigative equipment, they decided to experiment by setting up the devices in the hopes of capturing the phenomena. They watched and waited in anticipation of seeing the mysterious imprint appear for themselves, but nothing immediately transpired. As the room was fairly small, it was difficult to fit all of the twelve investigators in at the same time, so they broke up into two separate groups and took turns going in. Tina, Nancy, and Matthew were eager to capture at least some kind of paranormal activity on their equipment, so Matthew began using the tape recorder to see if he could collect any EVPs. After a few moments passed, the team asked one another whether they should now let the next group into the room. Tina jokingly replied *no,* which caused Nancy and Matthew to laugh out loud. On playing the tape recorder back, at the precise moment of Tina saying "no," an EVP of a woman's voice is heard saying *Get Out!*

As the second group entered the room, the guide took the current group further down the hallway into another guest room. Here the guide told of how most of the people who have stayed in this particular room would hear frequent knocking at the door, and thought it to be room service or even the maid, but as soon as they opened the door not a soul was in sight. Another experience was that while they were sleeping, they would suddenly awaken to find the bed covers being pulled off them. It's interesting to mention here that during the team's second visit to Boulder Dam Hotel many months later, they purposefully planned to stay in this very room to see if they too would experience the bed covers being pulled off for themselves, and even though Tina managed to stay awake all night to see if it would happen and really wanted to experience it happening, nothing transpired.

After the second group had caught up with them, they all decided to go back to the first guest room where they had initially heard the EVP—to see if anything else paranormal would show itself. As they entered the room their eyes were drawn directly to the bed, where they were shocked to see the appearance of the imprint of someone having just sat on the bed. Luckily, the video recorder that was previously set up by Tina had captured this phenomenon at the precise moment that it happened. The trainees, who were not used to experiencing any kind of paranormal occurrences unlike LVSSI, were now realizing—after hearing the EVP of the female voice demanding that they get out and witnessing the bodily imprint on the bed—that they were truly convinced of a spirit presence in the room and that Boulder Dam Hotel was definitely haunted.

The guide now took them down the back stairs of the hotel, which led them to a basement area where there was a room that appeared to be an equipment room. The room itself was quite cluttered, and Nancy thought it would be a good idea if they now did a 'control' experiment in here. She took a sheet of paper and a coin, traced the outline of the coin on the paper, placed the coin in the middle of the circle, and then hid the paper behind some equipment where no one would see it. The team then openly invited any spirit present in the room to move the coin from the circle if it wanted to; they then left the room and the guide locked the door behind them. She explained that she didn't want any other hotel visitors mistakenly walking into the room as it was full of various equipment, and neither did the team as they wanted no one touching their experiment.

They now wandered further into the basement where there were various meeting rooms located, and felt the distinct presence of someone following them down the hallway. As Tina turned to talk with Nancy, from the corner of her eye she noticed a shadow person.

"Did you see that?" Tina asked, saying, "From the corner of my eye I distinctly saw the shadow of a man following us."

Tina knew it was the shadow of a man because of the outline of his body and the physicality of his broad shoulders. It was difficult to see his face, but she could definitely see it from her peripheral view. To make sure that they weren't imagining things and that it wasn't their own shadows playing tricks on them, the team performed a few tests among themselves by having some members of the group stand at one end of the hallway, and others at the opposite end, and then they would all meet in the middle. Not one shadow belonging to any of them was seen by any of the twelve investigators, but soon afterwards everyone definitely saw the shadow person appear again...just as Tina had initially seen him.

At this point, the guide became really scared at what she had just witnessed and decided that she was no longer going to hang around in the basement with the team. Before leaving them to go back to her desk in the lobby, she gave them directions of how to get back to the main level. Feeling somewhat abandoned by her leaving suddenly, the team continued with their investigation alone, and headed further down the hallway where there were a couple of bathrooms, both male and female. They took a few moments to stop and use them, and after making sure that the lights were switched off, they continued with their investigation further down the hallway.

They found quite a large meeting room with a number of tables and chairs, and went inside to rest for a few moments before moving on. As they sat in the darkness, within moments they began seeing a multitude of orb activity—perfectly solid light orbs passing before their eyes one after the other. The trainees were getting extremely excited by what they were now seeing, and as Tina, Nancy, and Matthew's attention now became focused on them and their new orb experience, unfortunately they didn't manage to capture any of the orb activity on film.

However, they later discovered that the well-known celebrity, Howard Hughes, had frequently held meetings in this room and conducted a lot of his own personal business there. Apparently, he even once stayed in the hotel for several weeks after crashing his airplane at Lake Mead. The team raised questions about the orbs they had seen, and if it was possible that the orb activity had a connection with the spirit of Howard Hughes himself, as his presence once graced the room on numerous occasions when he was alive. Of course there was no definitive answer to this, but only the possibility.

Moving on out of the room and further down the hallway, where they had spent a considerable amount of time investigating and conducting a number of ghost experiments after seeing the shadow person, they noticed a fairly small room that had a closet in it. They witnessed strange flashes of light resembling that of shooting stars. These flashes of light only happened three or four times at the most and then abruptly stopped, and as no more activity was presenting itself in this room, they all decided to go back to the original part of the hotel.

Walking back along the hallway, they passed the bathrooms and they happened to notice that the light was on in the ladies' bathroom from underneath the door. They went in to see if anyone was in there and were surprised to see it was empty, and yet they distinctly remembered switching off the light after previously being in the room. They couldn't explain why the light should be on, as no one else was in that vicinity with them during the investigation.

As they made their way back to the stairway to take them to the original part of the hotel, Nancy began suddenly experiencing a choking sensation and was finding it very difficult to breath. She kept repeating, "I've got to get out of here, I've got to get out," and as she made her way onto the landing area, the choking feeling immediately started to subside. Interestingly enough, the team later discovered that there had once been a fire that had broken out in that exact location where Nancy had experienced the breathing problem. Clearly, she was reliving the past memory of it from a long time ago.

Once they reached the main level of the hotel where they had initially met the tour guide, they approached her at the desk and asked if she could unlock the door to the equipment room so that they could retrieve the control experiment that Nancy had put together. She obliged, and as they made their way back down to the basement and into the equipment room, they discovered that the coin had indeed been moved from out of the circle on the paper. The door to this room had been locked throughout the entire night's investigation, and so no one could have possibly entered the room at any time. This was solid proof to the team that there had to have been the presence of a spirit with them, and as they had invited *it* to move the coin, the spirit obviously acknowledged their request.

The Boulder Dam Hotel has acquired new ownership a number of times since LVSSI carried out their investigation, and not so long ago they approached the current owners to ask if they could continue with their investigation there. Unfortunately the new owners turned them down, as they did not want any publicity at the hotel. They also admitted to LVSSI that they did not believe in ghosts and did not want ghost hunters invading their property.

Conclusion

It's well known that old buildings can and do attract ghost activity due to the history that's associated with them. If LVSSI had been given another opportunity to re-investigate the Boulder Dam Hotel, I believe that they would have encountered much more paranormal phenomena there.

However, there were three solid pieces of evidence that did arise from the investigation—the EVP, the film footage of the mysterious imprint located on the bed, and photographs of orb phenomena. Although some of the orb activity was captured on camera, LVSSI was not able to photograph the multitude of orb activity that was experienced in the meeting room, as their attention was fully focused on the large group of trainees at the time.

Their experience of the shadow person was indeed very real, and each and every one of the team that night had witnessed its presence in the hallway of the basement. As for the control experiment that Nancy had put together, this was definitive proof of a spirit being around them in the equipment room, as it acknowledged their request and showed proof of its presence by moving the coin from the circle on the paper.

If you ever have the chance to visit Boulder Dam hotel, my advice would be to take a long a video camera and a small recording device with you, just in case you're able to catch some of the ghostly phenomena that so many people have talked about, and experienced during many of their Boulder Dam visits.

Appendix

The Ghost Hunter's Prayers

Opening Prayer

Saint Michael the Archangel, Defend us in battle. Be our protection against the wickedness and snares of the Devil. May God rebuke him, we humbly pray, and do thou, O Prince of the heavenly host, By the Power of God, thrust into hell Satan and all *evil spirits* who wander through the world for the ruin of souls. **Amen**.

Closing Prayer

In the name of Jesus Christ, I command all human spirits to be bound to the confines of the cemetery. I command all inhuman spirits to go where Jesus Christ tells you to go, for it is He who commands you. **Amen**.

The Ghost Hunter's Glossary

There are many words that ghost hunters use in reference to ghosts and haunted places. You're probably familiar with most of these words, but some may be new or have different meanings when they refer to haunted places.

The following information is provided by author and ghost investigator, Fiona Broome, and appears in her book, *Ghosts of Austin, Texas*. For more information, visit http://hollowhill.com/.

Afterlife

One of several terms used interchangeably to refer to life after death. The word "afterlife" has been used since 1615, and is generic enough to use in almost any setting and culture. Other popular terms include "crossing over," "the Otherworld," and "the other side."

Aliens

Visitors from other planets. We differentiate aliens from visitors that live in parallel worlds, the Otherworld, or what's generally characterized as the afterlife. Some ghost hunters believe in UFOs and aliens; others don't. Generally, ghost hunters don't mix the two studies.

Anomaly

Something that is out of place and unexplained. In paranormal studies, this word refers to any phenomena that we cannot explain. Example: A lens flare in a photo is not an anomaly if you can see the light source that created it, but an orb that cannot be explained is an anomaly.

Apparition

Since the early seventeenth century, this word has referred to a ghost that seems to have material substance. If it appears in any physical form, including a vapor-like image, it may be called an apparition.

Banshee

From the Irish, bean sidhe, meaning female spirit. Most families with Irish ancestors have at least one banshee story, but many people are reluctant to discuss this subject. Her wail does not always mean death. She does not cause anyone to die and she's generally *not* a ghost.

Clearing, or Space Clearing

This is a process of ridding an area of lingering unpleasant energy. It does not "kill" a ghost. Space clearing encourages ghosts to cross over, or at least leave the haunted location.

Immediately after a space clearing, ghosts can be noisier or more hostile than usual. An effective space clearing may take three to five days to work. In the most haunted settings, it's usually necessary to repeat the space clearing several times.

Demons

Historically, this term has included deceased individuals. However, since the early eighteenth century, the word "demon" has referred to an evil spirit, sometimes more powerful than man, but less than Deity. Today, we generally do not use this term to indicate a deceased human being. The female demon, very rarely mentioned, is a demoness.

Demons and possessions are treated like UFOs and aliens. That is, most ghost hunters have an opinion about them, but they rarely discuss them in connection with hauntings. The "Amityville Horror" is one noted exception where the story seemed to include both ghosts and possessions.

Doppelganger

A concept made popular in the early nineteenth century, the doppelganger is the apparition, or double, of a living person.

★ *Dowsing rods*

These are usually single rods, split rods, or L-shaped wires or twigs. Some people dowse with pendulums, too. They're popularly used to locate water and oil wells, and to measure energy levels of many kinds. For ghost research, we usually use two L-shaped rods.

In ghost hunting, the investigator loosely carries one rod in each hand, and watches the movement of the rods. When the rods cross or splay wide apart, it usually indicates a haunted location.

It's easy to make your own dowsing rods from coat hanger wire. Cut the wire near the top, and again at the opposite end of the lower section. Do this with two different coat hangers to create two dowsing rods.

You can also purchase ready-made dowsing rods. Be certain that they're long enough for ghost research; the 16-inch length is recommended. Look for dowsing tools that glow in the dark. They're especially useful for ghost hunting.

Hold each one loosely in your hands with your arms extended or your elbows bent at a right angle. The rods should be pointed straight ahead of you, and able to swing on their own.

If the rods are drifting, this could be from the normal movement of your body. However, in haunted places, the pull on the rods is strong and cannot be mistaken for a casual, unconscious movement of your hands.

When you step out of the haunted area, the rods return to their original position.

Some researchers successfully use dowsing rods to find unmarked graves. With practice, it's possible to use the rods to detect other information about the body in the grave and the spirit that may haunt the site.

Ectoplasm

Often referred to as "ecto," this is the physical residue of psychic energy. It's the basis for "slime" used in the "Ghostbusters" movies. Ectoplasm can be seen by the naked eye and is best viewed in dark settings, since it is translucent and tends to glow. It is very unusual.

★ *EMF*

The initials stand for Electro Magnetic Field, or Electro Magnetic Frequency. In the broadest terms, EMF is a combination of electrical and magnetic fields. You'll find EMF around power sources, fuse boxes, electrical outlets, computer monitors, microwave ovens, etc.

It's smart to study EMF so that you'll recognize the normal sources of elevated EMF readings. Constant, clearly defined EMF fields usually have a logical explanation.

Unexplained EMF fields may indicate something paranormal. EMF fields can be measured with various tools, including an EMF meter or a hiking compass.

Entity

An entity is any being, including people, animals, and ghosts. It can also refer to aliens, faeries, mystical beasts, and a wide range of paranormal creatures. If you use this term—and many ghost hunters do—be sure that others understand your context.

ESP

ESP is the abbreviation for Extra Sensory Perception. It means the ability to perceive things beyond the usual five senses of smell, hearing, touch, taste, and sight—and is often referred to as the "sixth sense."

★ ***EVP***

Electronic Voice Phenomena, or the recording of unexplained voices, usually in haunted settings. Sometimes the voices are heard during the investigation. More often, the voices are whispers, understood only when a sound recording is processed, filtered, and amplified with a computer.

When people first recorded EVP, they insisted on total silence so normal noises and talking wouldn't be confused with EVP. More recently, people have deliberately included sounds such as normal talking, white noise, and so on. Some researchers believe that ghosts may need ambient noise to create their own sounds and speech.

Most researchers use digital recorders to save EVP. Once the researcher is at home, he or she uses a computer program to filter out everyday noises, such as airplanes and passing cars. The recording may need to be speeded up or slowed down, or a range of sounds magnified above others.

Faeries

Beings that live in the Otherworld or Underworld, parallel to our world and not far from it. Many researchers who readily accept the reality of ghosts don't believe in faeries. Similar to the subject of aliens and UFOs, it's best to keep faerie research clearly separated from ghost hunting.

Fear

Most ghost hunters have a healthy respect for ghosts and paranormal phenomena. Many ghost hunters enjoy a "good scare." However, if you feel genuinely alarmed or frightened while ghost hunting, it's prudent to leave that location. It may have been your imagination, but there may be something (or someone) truly dangerous nearby.

Ghost hunting should always be interesting, and sometimes entertaining. If it's not, you may be at risk. Ghost hunting should never become a "dare" or an endurance test.

★ *Ghost*

A sentient entity or spirit that visits or lingers in our world, after he or she lived among us as a human being. We've also seen evidence of ghostly animals and pets.

Ghoul

This word has been mistakenly used to mean a ghost. "Ghoul" comes from Middle Eastern lore, where it may refer to an evil spirit that robs graves.

★ *Haunted*

Describes a setting where ghosts, poltergeists, and/or residual energy seem to produce significant paranormal activity. The word "haunt" originally meant to frequent.

Medium

This word usually refers to something in the middle, relative to size or duration. In ghost hunting, it means anyone who is able to convey communications from departed spirits. That is, the person is able to maintain a position between the world of the living and those who've crossed over, and talk with (or for) those on the other side.

This term was popularized in the mid-nineteenth century and is often used interchangeably with the word "psychic." Some people call themselves psychic mediums because they can communicate with the other side, but also sense other paranormal energy and/or work with ESP.

Occult

From the Latin, meaning something that is concealed or covered. Since the sixteenth century, it has meant anything that is mysterious. Today in America, it generally refers to magical, mystical, and experimental studies.

★ Orb

An orb is a round, whitish or pastel-colored translucent area in photos. Generally, these are perfectly circular, not oval. Many researchers believe that they represent spirits or ghosts.

If you're using a digital camera, it's important to differentiate between an area of broken pixels (called an "artifact") and the translucent, circular image that is an orb. Also, any reflective surface or light source can create a lens flare that looks like an orb. When taking photos, note glass, shiny metal, reflective signs, polished surfaces such as tables, headstones, and lights.

In most cases, ghost hunters do not see orbs when they're at a haunted site. Usually, orbs show up only in photos. They are the most common evidence for hauntings.

★ Ouija

From the French and German words for "yes," this is a spelling board used with a planchette. The device is intended to communicate with the spirit world, obtaining answers to questions.

Generally, we don't recommend them on serious ghost investigations. Some people are vehemently opposed to Ouija boards. The biggest problem is that researchers can't tell who is really moving the planchette. Even if it is a ghost, the spirit could be playing a prank or lying; the information from Ouija boards is unreliable for ghost research.

★ Paranormal

The prefix, "para," indicates something that is irregular, faulty, or operating outside the usual boundaries. So, "paranormal" refers to anything outside the realm and experiences that we consider normal.

Parapsychology

The study of mental abilities and effects outside the usual realm of psychology. Parapsychology includes the study of ESP, ghosts, luck, psychokinesis, and other paranormal phenomena.

Pendulum

A small weight at the end of a cord or chain that is usually about six to ten inches long. The movement of the weight, when uninfluenced by other factors, can be used to detect areas of paranormal energy.

Poltergeist

From the German meaning "noisy ghost," this term has been in use since the early nineteenth century to mean a spirit that makes noise, or otherwise plays pranks...usually annoying. Unlike other ghosts, poltergeists can move from one location to another, following the person they've chosen to torment. Many psychologists believe that poltergeists are not ghosts at all, but some form of psychokinesis or remote activity.

Portal

Literally, a doorway or gate; this term suggests a specific location through which spirits enter and leave our world. When there are multiple phenomena in a confined area, such as an abundance of unexplained orbs, some people call this a "ghost portal."

Possession

When an entity attempts to take control of a body that does not belong to them, it's called a possession.

In ghost hunting, this phenomenon is rare, but some psychics and mediums allow ghosts to speak through them. Sometimes, this can enable the living to communicate directly with the ghost and help him or her to cross over.

In extreme cases, a spirit can maliciously attempt to take over an unwilling person's body. Most ghost hunters will never witness this kind of possession, though it's a popular scene in horror movies. Unwilling possession is often linked to demonic activity.

Proof

There is no "proof" of ghosts when someone is a committed skeptic. People who won't believe in ghosts find other explanations for all scientific evidence of hauntings. A profound, personal encounter with a ghost or the unexplainable is the only way to change someone's mind about haunted places.

★ *Protection*

Some researchers use objects, rituals, routines, or specific processes to protect themselves against ghostly, demonic, or paranormal intrusions and effects. This is a personal matter, rarely discussed during a ghost hunt.

When you go on a ghost hunt, it's generally smart to carry something that you feel may protect you from evil. Most ghost hunters wear a small cross, Star of David, pentacle, or other religious jewelry. They often conceal it under clothing, or wear it as a ring, earrings, or on a bracelet where it won't be noticed.

Psi

"Psi" or "psy" is a popular term used to mean any psychic phenomena or psychic abilities that is sometimes inclusive of paranormal disturbances.

Psychic

From the Greek word meaning "of the soul," or of life (Paul used it in I Cor ii, 14), this word usually refers to the world outside the domain of physical law.

"Psychic" can relate to the spirit or the mind, depending upon the context. When someone is described as a psychic, it usually means that he or she is able to perceive things that are outside traditional physical laws and perceptions.

Psychical

A British term used as an adjective or adverb, for what Americans call "psychic."

Psychokinesis or Psycho Kinesis

To move something with the powers of one's mind. It may be a factor in some hauntings, and particularly in poltergeist phenomena. It's usually called "PK."

★ *Residual Energy*

Many ghost hunters believe that emotionally-charged events leave an imprint or residue on the physical objects nearby.

What distinguishes residual energy from an active haunting is that the energy/impressions repeat consistently, as if on a tape loop. The energy level may increase or decrease, but the content remains the same with each manifestation. By contrast, in an active haunting, the ghost may respond to environmental stimuli and direct contact.

Sixth Sense

Since normal phenomena are detected with the five senses (smell, taste, touch, hearing, and sight), anything that you experience outside those five senses may be categorized as a sixth sense. Usually, this indicates psychic detection or ESP.

Since M. Knight Shyamalan's movie of the same name, people usually think that the sixth sense refers primarily to seeing ghosts. In reality, few people see ghosts as full figures or living people.

In ghost hunting, the sixth sense can include everything from the ability to hear ghosts whispering, to an internal visual image from the past, or even a "creepy feeling" that can't be explained.

★ *Spirit*

This word comes from the Latin, meaning that which breathes. It means that which animates life, or the soul of the being.

Table Tapping, Table Tipping

A method to communicate with spirits. Usually, several people sit around a table with their hands on it, or holding hands on top of the table. Then, they ask the spirits to communicate by tapping on the table, perhaps once for yes and twice for no.

Others are successful in asking the ghosts to lift the table very slightly to show that they are present. Then, the ghosts may tap their replies, move a Ouija-type platen, or use some other means to communicate with movement around the table.

Tarot

The history of the Tarot deck is still unclear. However, since its use in fourteenth century Italy, "Tarot" refers to playing cards that are also used for fortune-telling or divination.

Telekinesis

From a Greek word meaning any motion that is activated from a distance. Technically, this could describe a remote-controlled toy boat, so most people use the word psychokinesis for ghost research.

Vortex

Since the time of Descartes, this has indicated the rotation of cosmic energy around a central point or axis. Beginning in the mid-nineteenth century, the word "vortex" has meant any whirling movement of energy or particles. Some people use this term to explain lines or narrow cylinders that appear highlighted in ghost photos.

Guidelines for Ghost Hunters

The following information is provided by author and ghost investigator, Fiona Broome and appears in her book, Ghosts of Austin, Texas. For more information, visit http://hollowhill.com/.

1. **Use common sense**. If your "gut feeling" indicates that you're in danger, leave immediately. Ghost hunting shouldn't be dangerous, nor should it be an endurance test.

2. **Never trespass**. If the site has "no trespassing" signs or looks as if it's closed, don't go in. Don't risk being arrested.

3. **Never go alone**. Take a friend with you when you go ghost hunting. Never go to a quiet or deserted site alone, and never explore risky neighborhoods on your own.

4. **Dress for the setting**. Sturdy shoes are vital, especially if you're outdoors, or if you have to run to get away from a ghost.

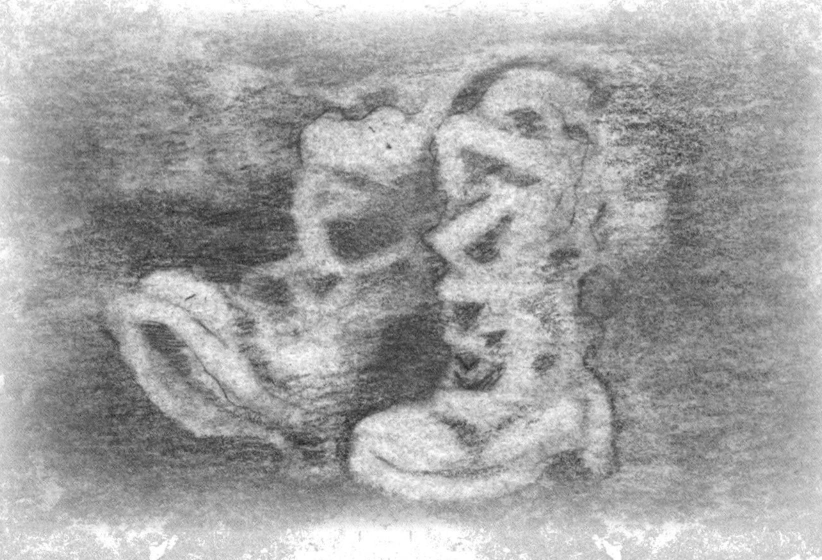

5. **Research the location**. Before visiting a location after dark, see it in the daylight to check for hazards, and things that might confuse you in lower light conditions.

6. **Respect the ghost and/or haunted location**. Never joke around cemeteries or other haunted locations. That seems to offend the ghosts, and they can retaliate. Or, they may become obstinate and refuse to manifest.

7. **Ghosts generally don't look "dead."** Few ghosts appear as full figure apparitions. When they talk, it's often a garbled whisper. That's why we record their "voices" to study more carefully, later.

8. **Interact with the ghosts as if they're alive**. Be polite; they usually consider the location their personal property. Don't command them to manifest in a specific way. Unless they're ghosts of actors, they won't usually perform for anyone on cue.

9. **Ghosts don't follow you home**. If you're troubled by unwanted thoughts or feel uneasy after a ghost hunt, call a friend, play your favorite music, or watch a funny TV show or movie. If the dark thoughts continue, consult your minister or spiritual advisor.

10. **Keep detailed notes about your ghost hunts**. Later, you'll find these notes very helpful, especially if you want to re-visit those haunted sites.

Endnote

LVSSI is happy to assist residents of the Las Vegas area if they are experiencing any unwelcome ghostly activity. You can reach them at their website, www.lvssi.org, or contact Tina Carlson directly at tina.carlson@lvssi.org.

The author is interested in interviewing any witnesses of, and people who have experienced, paranormal activity. Please contact her at the website www.letstalkparanormal.com or her email address, Lets_talkparanormal@yahoo.com

Resources

www.coasttocoastam.com

www.harrisinterative.com

www.lvssi.org

www.maryannghostbuster.com

www.vanpraagh.com